ACTS OF ACKNOWLEDGEMENT GLOSSARY

PAULINE SCHIAPPA

authorHOUSE®

AuthorHouse™
1663 Liberty Drive
Bloomington, IN 47403
www.authorhouse.com
Phone: 1 (800) 839-8640

Published by AuthorHouse 09/20/2019

ISBN: 978-1-7283-2834-8 (sc)
ISBN: 978-1-7283-2832-4 (hc)
ISBN: 978-1-7283-2833-1 (e)

Library of Congress Control Number: 2019914721

GLOSSARY

ACTS OF SPEECH AND ACTS OF KNOWLEDGE WORDS THAT REQUIRE INDIVIDUAL PERSONAL MEANING AND VALUE

Abeyance, "to place in abeyance," exists as a conceptual idea suggested by Georg Wilhelm Friedrich Hegel, (1770-1831), within his notions of "nodal line" and "measure" in consideration of dialectical cognitive process toward resolving contradictions that come to exist in human Mind Life metaphysical thought as the result of interaction between practical intellect (Hegel" Objective Mind) and abstract intellect (Hegel's Subjective Mind). "To place in abeyance" becomes metaphysical thought along "nodal line" suspended in human Mind Life between "a posteriori" practical intellect and "a priori" abstract intellect which "takes pause" in cognitive order to reflect upon possibility toward confident cognitive validation of earthly reality quality percepts coming to transcendentally transform into human Mind Life absolute truth concepts resulting as "a priori" knowledge in abstract intellect. "Mental pause" within metaphysical thought "puts into abeyance" earthly reality thought "within time suspended, when there "seems" to exist "nothing certain" provoking a transcendental transformation effecting that "earthly reality nothing uncertain" can become "something absolute" "suddenly," and, "sufficiently."

Absolute Truth: An earthly reality existence cannot know Absolute Truth; earthly human only seeks truth. Earthly human observes, learns, internalizes Nature Nature's everlasting universal laws that govern cosmic universe: earthly human observes, learns, and internalizes earthly social and political behaviors which earthly human Mind Life may conceptualize into absolute categories as moral or ethical, non-moral or non-ethical, earthly reality social behavior. Earthly human can only "know that which earthly human believes to be true" within an earthly human personal, idiosyncratic system of reality, system of truth, and system of belief. These personal, idiosyncratic systems of reality, systems of truth, and systems of belief enable psychological earthly human, psychological ego psyche, psychological mental stability toward interaction with earthly reality, allowing earthly human to ignore human Mind Life innate "a priori" metaphysical awareness.

Abstract intellect exists within human Mind life cognitive mental operations as that status of Abstract Intellect when Abstract Intellect is attempting to abstractly, conceptually facilitate quality of Practical Intellect ego psyche with earthly reality. Abstract Intellect has acquired metaphysical awareness quality within the cognitive operations of conscience conscious awareness, cognitive awareness, comprehension, understanding, and reason. Practical Intellect acquires personal and idiosyncratic earthly reality social awareness. Abstract Intellect continually attempts quality of cognitive mental operational validation, as well as, quality of psychological resolution, and, a quality of social awareness by means of human Mind Life cognitive structure, and, cognitive functions.

Abstraction exists as cognitive functional possibility of an essential human Mind Life conscience conscious awareness of metaphysical innate "a priori" concepts, or, spirit ideas, (sublime pro formational innate human Mind Life knowing), which, when recognized and realized by human Mind Life transcendently "trans form" into abstraction as absolute necessary concepts (sublime human Mind Life innate pro forms) which, (1) provoke human Mind Life to cognitively function (think), (2) enable human Mind Life to cognitively function (think), (3) separate physical earthly reality phenomenal social awareness into Hunan Mind Life Noumena metaphysical awareness, in cognitive order, in attempt to think in cognitive order to discover an absolute truth.

Absurdity comes to exist within human Mind Life mental status, at a given earthly time in a given earthly space in a given earthly reality, when Hunan Mind Life Abstract Intellect cannot "conceive" sufficient and adequate intellectual evidence in cognitive order to resolve the contradictions occurring between that which human Mind Life Abstract Intellect is able "to absolutely conceive" with that which psychological ego psyche is presently "perceiving" of phenomenal, uncertain earthly reality. Abstract Intellect cannot come to validate psychological ego psyche with present human Mind Life innate "a priori" knowledge in cognitive order to resolve meaningfulness in cognitive order to resolve psychological satisfaction within cognitive satisfaction.

Accommodation exists within mental operations as human Mind Life cognitive awareness that recognizes potentially meaningful and valuable schema and accepts newly recognized schema into already realized "a priori" innately existing schema.

Acts of information exist within earthly human Paratactical Intellects mental operations limited to practical intellect limited by an inferential or an inductive perceptual decision based and biased within an immediate contextual earthly reality situation void of human Mind Life cognitive awareness, cognitive reflection, cognitive resolution, and cognitive validation.

Acts of knowledge potentially come to exist within human Mind Life mental operations within mental moments that trans space "a priori" knowledge into acts of speech or acts of the written word "abstractly-filled" with human Mind Life recognized, realized, acknowledged, believable knowledge. Metaphysical Knowledge awareness transforms itself into earthly reality physical language. Within cognitive mental moments that transform human Mind Life "a priori" knowledge into earthly reality physical language, an act of knowledge pro forms and an act of language.

Acts of speech force pro form two potential qualities of earthly human verbal expression: acts of information or acts of knowledge.

Acts of language force pro form verbal or written expressions of acts of knowledge or acts of speech.

Actuality exists as the fulfillment of a potentiality.

Acumen exists as human Mind Life cognitive mental ability within cognitive mentally operational capability of insight that enables earthly human to effect the potentiality to intellectually assess and to cognitively validate with existing "a priori" knowledge the possibility of a meaningful measure of a perception, an impression, an opinion of an earthly reality contextual situation in cognitive order for earthly human to effect and to affect a meaningful measure from human body substance sense experience of earthly reality merely precariously socially aware of the experience as quality of a perception, an impression, an opinion of earthly reality toward cognitive attempt to acquire cognitive comprehension and cognitive understanding force pro forming cognitive intellectually evident confidence.

Adaptation exists within human Mind Life mental operations as cognitive awareness that resolves the contradictions existing between practical intellect existing as perceptual awareness of relative earthly reality with abstract intellect's intellectual evidence innately "a priori" existing in human Mind Life metaphysical awareness of essential categorical universals as prototypes and archetypes of existence, actuality, and essence of existence.

Adapting and surviving in the beginning, in the cradle, exists as quality of human Mind Life influence by human Psychological Life ego psyche mental operations driven by care to survive. In the beginning in the cradle the infant earthly human has not acquired sufficient knowledge or developed sufficient cognitive, concept, thought, language, and psychological development in cognitive order to have learned how to adapt and to survive using intellectual acumen, thus, infant earthly human relies upon egocentric thought and perceptual evidence in survival order to maintain earthy adaptation toward earthly survival.

Ad infinitum is a Latin term for "to infinity."

Aesthetic exists both empirically sentient and transcendentally metaphysical. Aesthetic exists both transcendentally empirical and transcendentally essential at the same time in the same space in the same reality (Jacques Derrida). Aesthetic exists as a metaphysical quality within human Mind Life cognitive mental operations toward the recognition and the realization of the beautiful. Aesthetic exists as a reasonable quality of cognitive mental operations because reason recognizes and realizes the beautiful. Human Mind Life mental operation of the quality of aesthetic reason recognizes and realizes both the empirically sentient and the transcendental beautiful at the same time in the same space in the same earthly reality. Aesthetic within mental operations brings forth a metaphysical attraction of the sentient transformed into the recognition and the realization of metaphysical beautiful. Aesthetic reasonably recognizes and realizes the good, the mysterious, the sacred, the profound. Plato suggested that the aesthetic realized in earthly reality became possible because of the "Forms" innately "a priori" held in human Mind Life. "We must assume behind this force the existence of a conscious and intelligent Mind. This Mind is the matrix of all matter."–Max Planck, <u>Das Wesen der Materie,</u> 1944. All created things are an imitation of their essential and eternal archetype (Jung). These essential archetypes exist eternal for humankind (Eliade).

Affecting exists as an ability of human Mind Life cognitive mental operations to enable cognitive influence of a certain quality of emotional consequence.

"A fortiori" exists as human Mind Life cognitive rhetorical argument... an "if-then" force pro formed stimulated reaction toward human Mind Life cognitive thought to cognitively react to earthly reality content and context.

Sense experience occurs because human body substance came to exist in earthly reality "a temporia." Human body substance, in social and in cognitive order to adapt and to survive in earthly reality "a temporia," possesses five physiological mechanisms (senses) in cognitive order to have sense experience with earthly reality. This phenomena exists fortitudinous toward possibility of human existence. If "self" comes to recognize and to realize earthly human tangible existence in earthly reality, self comes to be provoked... an "if-then" stimulated reaction. If "self" continues to rely upon something outside of himself to establish self's system of reality, system of truth, and system of belief___that government, religion, science, can come to tell earthly human truth, earthly human never "comes to know something actual," "self continues to know no thing!" Earthly human may come to know "earthly anything uncertain" by means of "a fortiori," "an if-then" force pro formed perception of earthly reality continuously validated by another perception of earthly reality always remaining without possibility of validation, always remaining within relative context and content of earthly reality situational existence.

Alchemy exists as the esoteric practice of faith and of hope in the Intelligent Design of both Nature Nature and Human Nature. If there exists the earthly real, then what is the purpose of the human in it, and, if there does not exist the earthly real, then, what is the purpose of the human in it. Alchemy exists as an esoteric investigation of knowledge as a system of reality and as a system of belief that in seeking knowledge "truth" may be found. Alchemy exists as the practice of faith and and of hope that human Mind Life cognitive reason can come to know the Intelligent Design of Human Nature.

Ambiguous exists in human Mind Life mental operations as a mental status of cognitive dissonance existing between perceptual awareness and cognitive awareness.

Analysis defines human Mind Life mentally operational process within logical thought of abstractly "deconstructing" the logical proposition into its constituent parts in cognitive order to discern the "essential" attributes and qualities necessary to make up the "actual" possibility (existence) of the abstract idea.

Analytic "a priori" propositions, as proposed by Gottlob Frege, (1848-1925), are statements of thought that require mathematical validation that would be based upon a mathematical language that made no reference to words "naming" (nouns) objects or people, and, that did not depend upon any "sense" (perception of experience) of the statement. Linguistic "sense" of a linguistic synthetic statement necessarily needed to "refer" to "naming" (nouns) by means of words. Mathematical language needed to void itself of all normative linguistic "sense" (perception) of a linguistic synthetic statement and all "denotation" by use of words (nouns) in cognitive order that there would not be any perceptual inference derived from the analytic a priori logical proposition. By voiding an analytic a priori proposition of any inferential referencing and any connotation of the linguistic "sense" of the proposition, the proposition could be validated mathematically linguistically "a priori" analytic. Frege argued that there could be no such thing as a "synthetic a priori logical proposition." A logical proposition could not use both deduction reasoning and induction reasoning within the same logical proposition and be considered "true." According to Frege, in cognitive order for a logical proposition to be considered as "true," the "logical" proposition by virtue of "logical thought a priori," must not come to mentally operationally validate itself by means of anything "synthetic." For Frege analytic a priori propositions were "true" because an analytic a priori proposition, using only mathematical language, no normative natural language, no "prescribed language systems," no sense perception, would disallow any possibility of disambiguation.

Analytic "a posteriori" synthetic propositions become statements of thought expressed by means of "formal" logical language or mathematical symbol system that can validate the synthetic proposition "a posteriori." An analytic "a posteriori" synthetic proposition does not rely upon sense perception of sense experience for its justification. An analytic "a posteriori" synthetic proposition can be validated by means of observed earthly reality, however, sense experience and sense perception are not bases for its truth justification. An analytical "a posteriori" synthetic proposition relies upon human Mind Life logical reason and/or logical reasonable mathematical symbol system toward "thought" validation toward a possibility of an earthy reality human Mind Life metaphysical thought. An example of an analytic "a posteriori" proposition states: "All bachelors are unmarried." An analytic "a posteriori" proposition is a statement whose predicate concept is contained within its subject content. The predicate validates the subject.

Practical Intellect, reinforced by Abstract Intellect, cognitively recognized and realized the validity of the analytic "a posteriori" proposition. The "a posteriori" proposition remained as quality of synthetic because (1) the proposition is earthly reality defined by earthly reality observation of an unmarried man, then, (2) physically linguistic defined as "a bachelor"____conditioned upon an earthly reality linguistically defined "word definition."

Abstract concepts, in the form of "a priori" knowledge, validate new analytic propositions, new synthetic "a posteriori propositions", and, new synthetic "a priori" propositions, and, analytic "a priori' propositions by means of deductive reasoning using metaphysical knowledge "a priori." Analytic propositions suggest "truth" by virtue of linguistic symbol meaning which earthly reality system of truth was bestowed upon quality of truth via cognitive validation by means of metaphysical "a priori" knowledge innately held in human Mind Life. Human Mind Life innately "a priori" knows absolute concepts____there are men, there are unmarried men, unmarried men are "name word" bachelors. Earthly reality logical, inferential induction due to human Mind Life logical reasonable deduction.

Analytical proposition, according to the Logical Positivists' philosophy of science, is a statement of thought expressed by means of using a specific, pre-determined, scientifically "formal" language which could come to "disallow" any ambiguity in meaning toward validation "a posteriori" synthetically. An analytical proposition would be "limited" to using "ideal-language analysis" or "formal definition defining and describing the specific functions of a discipline without ever alluding to any ontological, epistemological, or metaphysical meanings. Ontological, epistemological, and metaphysical statements cannot be verified by empirical data, therefore, become meaningless. Analytical propositions are restricted to the use of the meanings given to scientific terminology or to a symbol system which would be used by the practitioner of the discipline, and, these meanings did not necessary open themselves to any contradictions because of any other observable, empirical data. Analytical propositions had first been proposed by the Vienna Circle (1922). Bertrand Russell, (1872-1970), and Ludwig Wittgenstein, (1889-1951), were leading advocates devoted to a notion of a "unified scientific world conception," even writing a dictionary of scientific terms to be used in analytical scientific propositions that would define earthly reality. Logical positivists' analytical propositions were made true or false by means of pre-defined, specific, formal, scientific language. Logical positivists' analytical propositions would define and describe knowledge gained only "a posteriori" because any knowledge which may have been assumed to have been gained innately, metaphysical "a priori" from human Mind Life became meaningless. Use of an established earthly reality "formal" language within an analytical proposition voided any possibility of disambiguation because the form of the language used within an analytic proposition held "meaning" which related to only earthly reality facts about observed earthly reality. Intelligent Design interfered with such analytical "a posteriori" synthetic logic because human Mind Life has been intelligently designed to force pro form logical deductive reasoning. Human body substance needs to meet human Mind Life.

Anamnesis. The Greeks, especially Plato, discussed human Mind Life metaphysical concept of Anamnesis as a human Mind Life innate "a priori" absolute metaphysical awareness of truth (Human Nature innate nous as noesis). Human Mind Life existing as nous awareness of noesis, (1) innately "a priori" knows truth, (Noumena), (2) creating new knowledge from human Mind Life cognitive function of intellectually, cognitively understanding meaning and value from earthly reality sense experiences, (3) immediately spontaneously and autonomously recognized and realized as "there" existing in earthly reality as cognitive quality of intellectual intuition.

AntiPositivism exists as a notion in social science suggesting that social human behavior can best be investigated within "interpretive" "qualified" defined (as set group) observation. AntiPositivism was called "anti" "Positivism" because Positivism had maintained that social human behavior was best investigated by means of "quantifying" "real" "observable" social human behavior. Positivism had suggested that pre-determined, scientific, mathematical "formal" language could come to generically "logically" define social human behavior. Ferdinand Tonnies had suggested that the human phenomena could not be explained (understood) without using human Mind Life metaphysical concepts. Both Positivism and AntiPositivism disclaimed use of philosophical, metaphysical, and epistemological language within "scientific sociological" investigation and explanation of social human behavior. Scientific sociology uses "social scientific paradigms," which scientific sociology regard as truth.

"Anything" can come to exist within earthly reality sense perception of sense experience dependent upon (1) quality of environment, (2) quality of earthly rreality sense experience which is dependent upon earthly reality sense awareness provoking some quality of mental operations (thinking) by means of Practical Intellect ego psyche awareness, (3) Practical Intellect ego psyche awareness exists within human mental operations when "self" acquires mental ability to acquire mental awareness of "self" existing both tangibly as human body substance and intangibly as human Mind Life within only a perceived earthly reality, (4) Practical Intellect ego psyche awareness comes "to recognize and to realize" that "self" is a unique, personal, and idiosyncratic existence within a human body substance existing in a contextual, situational, relatively uncertain earthy reality. Practical Intellect ego psyche begins to "perceive" that a "nothing" could be an "anything uncertain," which ego psyche may perceive earthly reality nothing uncertain to be, (5) ego psyche can force pro form as the qualifier, as the facilitator, as the mediator of the possibility for the "nothing" not to become known as an "earthly reality uncertain anything," when the "nothing" must become known to human Mind Life as "Something Absolute" meaningful and valuable. How does this come to happen____Practical Intellect earthly reality quality of earthly reality acquired perceptual evidence transcendentally transforms quality of acquired perceptual evidence into human Mind Life quality of acquired knowledgable intellectual evidence innately known as "a priori" (Plato's sublime Forms) metaphysical awareness via the cognitive process of the comprehension toward cognitive process of the understanding. The Greeks, especially Plato, referred to transcendental cognitive transfer of earthly reality quality of sense intuition as human Mind Life process of metaphysical concept of Anamnesis in which human Mind Life metaphysical knowledge is recognized and realized, almost immediately, when sense perceiving.

"A posteriori" knowledge develops in human Mind Life within mental operational process of Practical Intellect interacting psychologically with ego psyche within earthly reality. (1) Human body substance sense experiences earthly reality acquiring a sense perception of earthly reality; (2) sense perception of sense experience requires facilitation and qualification by means of ego psyche quality of psychological thought. "Whatever" ego psyche is perceiving of the relative, contextual, immediate situational experience demands validation (resolution) provoked by that which Abstract Intellect "a priori" innately holds as believable intellectual evidence. In cognitive order for Abstract Intellect "to accept" as newly acquired knowledge from the sense perception of the sense experience, ego psyche's perception must be validated (resolved) with already existing "a priori" knowledge innately existing in human Mind Life. Initially "a posteriori" proposition comes to exist within Practical Intellect as a "percept." Once life experience by human body substance becomes a "perception," the "perception" comes to exist as a "synthetic a posteriori" proposition about life experience. Synthetic "a posteriori" proposition about life experience remains in human Mind Life mental operational status as "synthetic" because Practical Intellect demands Abstract Intellect to intellectually validate (resolve) the "a posteriori" synthetic proposition. Until Abstract Intellect intellectually validates (resolves) the "a posteriori" synthetic proposition, neither Practical Intellect nor Abstract Intellect can comprehend the synthetic "a posteriori" perception of sense experience as newly accepted recognized and realized "a priori" knowledge in human Mind Life. Practical intellect places the "synthetic a posteriori proposition" "in abeyance" within "mental moments" while Practical Intellect cognitively comprehensively interacts with Abstract Intellect. Within these "mental moments" the "synthetic a posteriori" proposition moves into mental operational status of a "synthetic a priori" proposition (possibility of believability). The "synthetic a priori" proposition transforms itself by means of the cognitive mental operations of cognitive awareness and cognitive comprehension toward possibility of intellectual validation (resolution) into newly accepted recognized and realized "a priori" believable knowledge via human Mind Life function of the comprehension.

Apperceive exists as a cognitive mental operation of assimilating and of integrating presently recognized and realized metaphysical concepts, almost immediately, into conscious awareness.

Application exists within mental operation as cognitive awareness that the schema already existing in cognitive structure possesses potentially meaningful attributes in cognitive order that these already existing schema, via thought thinking metaphysical thought, can transform, into human Mind Life cognitive acquisition of new schema that can transfer toward meaningful cognitive resolution.

Apprehension may come to exist within cognitive mental operations as a provocation toward cognitive mental awareness. Apprehension may exist within human Mind Life cognitive mental operations as a fear of cognitive mental awareness. Apprehension may exist within cognitive mental operations as an emotive reaction to cognitive mental awareness. Apprehension may occur within any of these three statuses of cognitive mental operations interaction with cognitive mental awarenesses when ego psyche Practical Intellect cannot come to cognitively interact with Abstract Intellect in cognitive order to cognitively satisfy cognitive mental awarenesses, or, psychological awarenesses, with present interaction amongst both qualities of intellects, Practical and Abstract, ego psyche, and earthly reality. Both Intellects apprehend that reality is winning!

"A priori" knowledge exists (1) innately within human Mind Life Abstract Intellect as quality of innate metaphysical knowledge "a priori," (2) existing innately within human Mind Life Abstract Intellect as "absolute universal concepts" of knowledge (Intellectual Design) which acquisition did not depend upon sense perception of sense experience of earthly reality, (3) became "recognized and realized" within human Mind Life Abstract Intellect by "a priori" cognitive process of human Mind Life mental operations transcendental transformation of synthetic "a posteriori" information acquired from the sense perception of sense experience as validated by human Mind Life innate "a priori" knowledge.

Arche exists as philosophical speculation brought forth by the Greek philosophers that there existed "ultimate prototypical, archetypical principles by which "all things" could be explained."

Archetypes represent conceptual universal prototypes and archetypes existing within the collective unconsciousness of humankind, within conscious, or, unconscious awareness. Human Mind Life cognitive mental operationally recognition and realization of prototypes ad archetypes enable human Mind Life mental operations to define the essential and necessary criteria of existence of Human Nature, by human Mind Life reason of necessary contingency, believable versus unbelievable, in cognitive order to come to know something Absolute. For Plato Archetypes represented themselves in a concept of "Forms" as cognitive mental "a priori" ideas which innately existed in human Mind Life. Sublime pro formational "Forms" existed necessarily contingently collectively in all human Mind Life in cognitive order that sublime pro formational universal metaphysical concepts existing within any individual Human Mind Life could come to cognitively coalesce Everyman's particular percepts observed of phenomenal earthly reality cognitively transcendently transformed into Everyman's universally necessary metaphysical awareness of Human Nature. For Carl Jung Archetypes came to inherently exist within the collective unconsciousness of humankind over time in space in earthly reality due to their quality of continuous abstractly recognized and abstractly realized use, consciously or unconsciously, as the universal comparative prototypes and archetypes of a "should be" earthly reality. For Carl Jung these Archetypes negatively or positively effected and affected psychological ego psyche earthly reality social behavior.

Argumentation theory is the study of informal logic's fallacies toward critically questioning sublime pro formational "a priori" Forms that relate to every day practical situations.

Assimilation exists within mental operations as the cognitive awareness that allows existing schema to include and to merge potentially meaningful and valuable schema into the existing schema.

Association exists within mental operations as the cognitive awareness that allows a potentially meaningful schema to assimilate with relevant schema already existing in cognitive structure establishing broader knowledge of earthly reality, which, earthly reality is apperceiving so autonomously and spontaneously. Associative schema cognitively avoids cognitive disassociation within cognitive learning.

Associative learning exists within mental operations in human Mind Life as cognitive awareness as learning (cognitively acquiring new knowledge) in which earthly human knowledge base is sufficiently stable to comprehend and to organize the relationship of potentially meaningful new learning, and, to attach the new learning to that relevant existing knowledge already existing within cognitive structure. Associative learning permits newly acquired schemas related to already acquired schemas the ability to recognize the commonalities of their essences, and, to assimilate the new schemas with the already existing schemas, thus preventing dissimulation within learning.

Associative sensation stimulates associative learning. Anyone or all of the five senses may provoke human Mind Life cognitive mental operations to "associate" that which sense experience is sense perceiving in cognitive order to attach cognitive intellectual value and meaning to the sense perception of a sense experience.

Attention exists within mental operations as cognitive awareness that Practical Intellect needs to coalesce with Abstract Intellect in cognitive order to focus cognitive awareness upon that which Practical Intellect believable knows exists as perceptual awareness of earthly reality and that which Abstract Intellect believably knows as metaphysical conceptual awareness of earthly reality.

Attitude becomes a mental status of a personal and idiosyncratic mental perception, impression, opinion of an observed earthly reality of a given situational context within a given time in space in earthly reality. This personal and idiosyncratic mental perception, impression, opinion cannot become cognitively validated with existing personal knowledge in cognitive order to cognitively effect a comprehensive understanding of the specific mental perception, impression, opinion because attitude is psychologically developed by ego psyche, place into Practical Intellect, and, not by human Mind Life Abstract Intellect as universal truth. This mental status of cognitive invalidation evokes a status of cognitive dissatisfaction and psychological dissatisfaction. Attitude may become a perceptual expression of self-consciousness. Attitude may affect the possibility toward mutual perceptual awareness and any possibility of a dialectical discussion amongst earthly humans____evoking a cognitive and a psychological disconnect amongst earthy humans. Carl Jung suggested two notions of ego psyche types____one as becoming extraverted, exaggerated ego psyche "attitude," and, the other, as becoming introverted cognitive "functions." Ego psyche may be an extraverted "attitude" as a perceptual reality establishing ego psyche as possessing a social set group value. Ego psyche may be an introverted cognitive "function" when ego psyche attempts to interact amongst earthly humans while sense perceiving lack of adequate intellectual evidence.

Attributes, existing within mental operations, exist innate toward potentiality of recognition and realization within metaphysical awareness. Attributes exist as essential qualities of being Human Nature. Attributes may come to be acquired as both physical prowess of human body substance, as well as, human Mind Life intellectual acumen.

Awareness, existing within mental operations, may exist as quality of sensual perception within Practical Intellect, or, as quality of knowledge in Abstract Intellect.

Awareness, existing within mental operations, may exist as quality of sensual perception within Practical Intellect, or, as quality of knowledge in Abstract Intellect. Awareness exists within Human Mind Life mental operations, both practical and abstract, as metaphysical abstraction. Conscious awareness exists as metaphysical abstraction of "whatever is going on" in either Practical Intellect or Abstract Intellect. If earthly human remains his entire life using only his Practical Intellect as a practical and a pragmatic interaction with earthly reality built upon inferential induction (which requires some quality of thought), an immediate impression of a contextual situation (which requires some quality of thought), an imitation of others behaviors or his previous successful behaviors (which requires some quality of thought), or, a mere mechanistic robot that reacts when stimulated, all sensual perceptions of life experiences, except the last example of human being as a mechanistic robot, demand some form of abstraction within a quality of thought. Whether earthly human "thinks" pragmatically sensible using only Practical Intellect, or, earthly human acquires the intellectual acumen to think conceptually about the ad infinitum possibilities of earthly reality, and, of human Mind Life, earthly human, in social and cognitive order to function in earthly reality must use abstract thought____perceptually or conceptually. A quality of conscious awareness of earthly human's life experiences, as well as of self, depends upon that "meaningful measure" earthly human develops as quality cognitive thought comes to exist as limited by sense perception of mere practical, pragmatic, and psychological Practical Intellect, or, unlimited potential conscience conscious awareness conception by Abstract Intellect.

Behavior exists as earthly human species organism mentally operational "a posteriori," as well as, "a fortiori," reaction to provocation by earthly reality stimuli. Behaviors can be conditionally learned coming to exist as repetitive, non-qualitatively, non-cognitively involved reactional habits as the result of repetitive same behavior reaction to earthly reality stimuli. Repetitive, imitative same behavior reaction to earthly reality stimuli result as socio-cultural norm-determined valued behaviors. Socio-cultural repetitive behaviors beget more socio-cultural repetitive behaviors____which beget repetitive, imitative socio-cultural stimulated behaviors. Behavior may come to exist as "a posteriori" expression of mentally operational spontaneous and ingenuously sagacious reaction as the result of qualitative cognitive functions' reaction to earthly reality stimuli due to quality of sense experience and human Mind Life creative reaction to sense experience (Anamnesis intellectual intuition). A behavior may come to be manifested as a new, never manifested before, spontaneous and ingenuously sagacious "a posteriori" reaction to earthly reality stimuli as Anamnesis intellectual intuition. Human Mind Life newly acquired "a priori" knowledge____newly acquired intellectual awareness____newly acquired cognitive awareness____newly acquired conscious awareness begets newly acquired spontaneous and creatively sagacious earthly reality behaviors.

Behaviorism exists as a modern psychological system of belief that, since science cannot discern human mental operations or human status of conscious awareness, the observation of human behavior becomes the only means by which to categorize, classify, and define the phenomena of earthly human activity interacting with the phenomena of earthly reality. Behaviorism proposes that earthly human behavior interacts with earthly reality void of intellect, psychological ego psyche, and free will. Intellect, ego psyche, and free will exist beyond earthly reality physical, and, science can only observe and document earthly reality physical. Contemporary system of belief in science, in the social sciences, and in secular humanism deny the metaphysical____deny human an intellect, an ego psyche, and free will. Contemporary system of belief in science, in the social sciences, in secular humanism suggest that earthly human behaviors exist as physical property of human body substance provoked, determined, and conditioned by physical stimuli existing outside body physical as empirical earthly reality phenomena. According to modern science "outside of human body substance" phenomenal material, object–determined earthly reality stimulates earthly human to behave. System of belief in modern psychology and in contemporary sociology suggest that it is material, physical earthly reality phenomena that provokes, determines, and conditions earthly human behaviors. Contemporary materialists simply deny any existence of the metaphysical, and, chose to overlook quantum physics. Quantum physics investigates the nature of matter interacting with energy, and, vice versa, energy interacting with matter. Quantum physics suggest that matter has far less "substance" than it has energy___that matter can only be maintained by inspiration of an invisible field energy. According to quantum mechanics the phenomena of physical behavior (not necessarily limited to human behavior) occurs due to inspiration of an invisible field energy resulting in aspirational attraction toward phenomena of behavior. "As a man who has devoted his whole life to the most clear headed science, to the study of matter, I can tell you as a result of my research about atoms this much: There is no matter as such. All matter originates and exists by virtue of a force which brings the particle of an atom to vibration and holds this most minute solar system of the atom together. We must assume behind this force the existence of a conscious and intelligent Mind. This Mind is the matrix of all matter." –-Max Planck, <u>Das Wesen der Materie,</u> 1944.

Being-for-itself exists in earthly reality as Human Nature being essence in existence.

Being-in-itself exists in earthly reality as ontic praxis-in-reality.

Belief (a belief) comes to exist within human Mind Life intellects as knowledge "a priori" after cognitive validation of a quality of earthly reality sublime pro formational information that has been mentally operationally transformed into intellectual evidence____consciously aware believed due to human Mind Life conscious aware recognition and realization of human Mind Life innate "a priori" sublime pro formations. Belief becomes human Mind Life knowledge. Knowledge must be cognitively believed before knowledge becomes quality of human Mind Life knowledge.

Belief is a mental operation by which earthly human cognitively acts upon earthly reality sublime pro formational information transforming earthly reality sublime pro formational information into accepted, personal knowledge cognitively validated with already existing innate "a priori" knowledge. *Belief* transforms by means of human Mind Life cognitive structure and cognitive functions that quality of earthly reality sublime pro formational information which an earthly human discerns as meaningful and valuable into acquired personally believable human Mind Life knowledge. *Belief,* as a cognitive mental quality, exists as a cognitive mental operational ability, as processes of cognitive structure and cognitive functions, to discern to transform that which may be possibly cognitively validated into that which becomes intellectually validated with existing innate "a priori" knowledge in cognitive order to will the expression of *belief* as behavior or as language, "in good faith." Earthly human knowledge must become believable to earthly human Mind Life, otherwise, that knowledge would have no meaning nor value for earthly human. *Belief* becomes a cognitive mentally operational ability to give metaphysical, epistemological meaning and value towards mental operation of conscious awareness of human Mind Life knowledge toward establishing a system of belief, a system of truth, a system of earthly reality. Sublime pro formational knowledge awareness exist innate "a priori" in human Mind Life. In cognitive e order for earthly human "to come to believe" human Mind Life innate "a priori" knowledge as human Mind Life innate "a priori" knowledge that possibly can be recognized and can be realized into earthly reality, human Mind Life must hold cognitive faculty toward a prolegomena toward acquiring metaphysical knowledge. Human Mind Life innately holds cognitive faculty toward metaphysical knowledge. Knowledge must be metaphysically believed before knowledge becomes knowledge.

Belief, when existing based within cognitive mentally operational ability of *Faith,* demands no scientific validation, no earthly reality stimulation. *Faith* exists as an innate "a priori" cognitive mentally operational ability to acquire intellectual and psychological confidence in necessary contingency principles as essential attributes as true and valuable toward accepting a system of belief upon metaphysical absolute, innate, "a priori" conceptual awareness of abstract concept of *Faith*_____ in necessary contingency principles which have been metaphysically cognitively recognized and realized as essential nature toward holding existence as Human Nature. *Faith,* existing as a mental status of cognitive confidence, establishes earthly human essential existence as system of reality, system of truth, and system of belief. Cognitive confidence accepting a system of belief has been established within a quality of cognitive awareness within a quality of conscious awareness. Regardless of quality of cognitive awareness of quality of conscious awareness, earthly human maintains *Faith* in earthly human system of reality, system of truth, and system of belief, otherwise, earthly human would go insane. Establishing and accepting a system of belief upon *Faith*, existing as cognitive confidence in metaphysically, cognitively realized necessary contingency essential principles, requires no psychological resolution and no psychological qualification because mentally operational ability of *Faith* has no psychological confidence in ego psyche's relationship with earthly reality when ego psyche's interaction with earthly reality has no interaction with human Mind Life Abstract Intellect. Abstract concept of Faith exists within human Mind Life metaphysical awareness_____metaphysical awareness recognized and realized by human Mind Life as essential sublime pro formational Human Nature.

Human Mind Life mentally operational ability of *Faith* confidently maintains the earthly human system of belief. Earthly human cognitively validates metaphysical awareness of system of belief with metaphysical awareness of essential Human Nature____as a sublime forced pro formance of Human Nature, itself for itself. *Faith* in Human Nature knowledge force pro forms earthly reality system of reality, system of truth, and system of belief regardless of "meaningful measure" of the quality of knowledge, or, the quality of cognitive awareness of conscious awareness. Due to "meaningful measure" of quality of knowledge within human Mind Life Abstract Intellect force pro forming within cognitive awareness within conscience conscious awareness, Abstract Intellect will chose to place in abeyance perceptual decisions made about earthly reality until earthly human psychological awareness can integrate personal awareness, intellectual awareness, and conscience conscious awareness toward ***renewed faith in system of belief.*** Theory, existing within dynamic state of theory, does not become belief until earthly human has cognitively intellectually validated present existing innate "a priori" knowledge with any earthly reality "a posteriori" sense experience, observation, experiment, or, inferential induction of earthly reality synthetic propositional theory toward possibility of inclusion of conclusion of the theory into system of belief. Belief, when existing as a mental ability of belief, is the mental process which transforms that which may be cognitively believable into that which has become intellectually believable by means of validation with present existing human Mind Life knowledge awareness. Belief, as a mental quality, is a mental operational ability to discern to transform that which could be possibly cognitively validated into that which has become intellectually validated with present existing "a priori" knowledge in cognitive order to will the expression of that belief into behavior or language, "in good faith." Earthly human knowledge must become believable to earthly human, otherwise, that knowledge would have no value, or, meaning for earthly metaphysical human Mind Life. Belief becomes a mentally operational ability to give metaphysical, epistemological value and meaningful measure towards human Mind Life believable knowledge awareness. Earthly reality information exists as quality of phenomenal earthly human perception, impression, and opinion. Earthly reality synthetic information does not exist as validated believable universally essentially principled conscious awareness of essence of Human Nature existence.

Bias comes to exist within mental operations as an act of prejudice because of lack of sufficient knowledge.

Body substance. Contemporary system of belief in science "believes" that there exists only one substance, which is physical substance.

Contemporary system of belief in science holds that there does not exist any metaphysical realm of existence human Mind Life essential existence. Body substance, according to contemporary system of belief in science, holds that earthly human body substance is physical possessing physical substance property and physical mental property (holding earthly reality phenomenal synthetic information.)

Brings forth exists as a metaphysical quality of human Mind Life cognitive mental operations forced pro formed to create knowledge and to linguistically elucidate that knowledge as well as to "worthily" behave that knowledge.

Categories exist innately as metaphysical concepts of the essential universals functioning in earthly reality metaphysically, cognitively recognized and realized by human Mind Life in cognitive order that earthly human maintains and sustains Human Nature within earthly reality as Human Nature "should be." Earthly human psychological ego psyche "behaves" within earthly reality as a selfish earthly reality social and political nature towards seeking self-satisfaction and self-gratification from phenomenal earthly reality that results in human ego psyche "behaving" psychologically selfish. Darwin's survival of the fittest____ psychological ego psyche "behaves" as a survival animal who lacks recognition and realization of human Mind Life conscious awareness of Hume Nature. Aristotle presented metaphysical awareness that there are four causes that bring forth effect upon earthly reality. These four causes reside as metaphysical essentials enabling effect upon physical earthly reality. The first cause, the Material Cause, suggests that there must exist a "raw" (physical) material in earthly reality order that "something actual" can exist; in Aristotle's view the material cause, because it could be "anything uncertain " existing in the physical realm, held a "potentiality" of being acted upon by a metaphysical intention of rational and aesthetic "worthiness." The second cause, the Formal Cause, existed as the metaphysical intention (human Mind Life cognitive mentally operational idea) of rational and aesthetic "worthiness" of the actuality of metaphysical possibility that earthly reality "anything uncertain" could, due to the force pro formance of human Mind Life, transcendently transform earthly reality phenomenal into earthly reality "should be." The third cause, the Efficient Cause, existed as the metaphysical, the rational, and the aesthetic, qualities of the potentiality of the human Mind Life actuality to force pro form earthly reality "anything uncertain" into earthly reality "something 'should be' actual." The Efficient Cause would, due to Human Nature necessary contingency, resides within the mental operational qualities of human Mind Life that brought forth the Final Cause. The Final Cause, for Aristotle, was the telos, or, the virtue of by reason why "something actual" came to exist. Charles Darwin suggested that evolution might be viewed as a process of a morphology; however Darwin suggested that within that morphology, of necessary contingency, there existed a teleological purpose. Ernst Mayr suggested that adaptation became the "a posteriori" result of an "a priori" goal-seeking of human Mind Life within earthly reality recognizing and realizing the metaphysical realm innately "a priori" existing as essential human Mind Life.

Cause and effect. Metaphysically and sentiently for every genesis of causation there will occur either an intended or an unintended effect.

Chaos comes to exist within mental operations when intellectual evidence cannot validate perceptual evidence as truth worthy thus bringing forth status both within mental operations, language, and behavior complexity, incongruity, disparity, absurdity, and anarchy.

Classic exists as the prototypical example of any idea or manifestation of an ideal. Greek and Roman civilizations have acquired prototypical classification in regards to categorizing worthy human manifestations in earthly time in earthly space in earthly reality.

Cognition exist as the mental operations and mental awarenesses existing within human Practical Intellect and human Abstract Intellect. Cognition develops as the result of meaningful symbolic (conceptual) learning within thought development, language development, concept acquisition, cognitive awareness, comprehension, understanding, as provoked by earthly reality perceptual awareness, which perceptual awareness involves an immediate content and context awareness from situational and intentional stimuli existing within earthly reality. If perceptual awareness (sense determined, dynamic and idiosyncratic awareness) does not effectively and affectively interact with conscious awareness (learned, acquired, personal, idiosyncratic, dynamic awareness), then the quality of perceptual awareness existing mentally operationally idiosyncratic, and, the quality of conscious awareness existing mentally operational idiosyncratic suffer by not allowing new conscious awareness to be acquired by earthly human. Perceptual awareness facilitates and qualifies cognition because perceptual awareness exists within mental operations as awareness of psychological quality of ego psyche's interactions with personal awareness, intellectual awareness, and conscious awareness. Cognition becomes the operation of mental processes involving abstracting ability to acquire percepts and concepts within human Practical and Abstract intellects. Intellect exists as that quality of mental operations and mental awarenesses acquired by means of the quality of concept, thought, language, cognitive development interacting with psychological development acquired through learning as well as the understanding, use, and expression of the interrelationships of these mental operations and mental awarenesses. Intellect is that quality of mental operations and mental awarenesses which enables acquisition of "synthetic a posteriori" knowledge. There exist two types of intellect within mental operations and mental awarenesses: Practical Intellect and Abstract iIntellect. Intellects interact with ego psyche within earthly reality.

Cognitive awareness exists as the discretionary mental operation of focusing attention upon the essence, the status, and the possibility of the actuality of a metaphysical concept. Cognitive awareness becomes earthly human discretionary mental operation of ability to focus attention, via thought, upon Human Nature earthly reality existence, the criterial qualities, and, temporary situational status of earthly reality, as well as, the possibility of the actuality of mentally, abstractly recognizing and realizing criterial archetypical and prototypical attributes as necessary contingency for Human Nature to actually exist in earthly reality. There are sub-processes occurring within the mental operation of cognitive awareness that meaningfully measure quality of cognitive awareness. These sub-processes include attention, associative learning, association, adaptation, accommodation, assimilation, and application. Cognitive awareness may be a function of perception, conceptualization, comprehension, understanding, and reasoning. Cognitive awareness exists as a self-awareness of an individual and idiosyncratic conscious awareness.

Cognitive awareness... conscious awareness.... conscious experience... personal consciousness... cognitive awareness commensurates human Mind Life cognitive attention as metaphysical thought thinking metaphysical thought provoking human Mind Life cognitive functions using cognitive structures. Conscious awareness initiates sense perception to cognitively interact with human Mind Life abstract conceptualization. Conscious awareness interacts with human Mind Life intellectual awareness interacts with ego psyche self awareness interacts with conscience consciousness. Conscience consciousness interacts with ego psyche interacting within earthly reality.

Cognitive awareness force pro forms sense experience conscious experience developing personal consciousness as unique persona force pro forming unique magnanimity behaving human personality expression into earthly reality. Conscience conscious awareness force pro forms ego psyche.

Cognitive bias, existing in mental operations, exists as a mental potentiality toward a possibility of a specific mentally operational outcome.

Cognitive compensation occurs within mental operations when there exists a lack, or void, of adequate cognitive structure and cognitive functions, as well as a lack, or void, of sufficient knowledge, in cognitive order to acquire a balance within the interaction amongst intellects, ego psyche, and earthly reality. Ego psyche, alone, facilitates, qualifies, processes earthly reality without cognitive validation from abstract intellect. Ego psyche compensates for cognition. Ego psyche processes earthly reality egocentrically relying upon practical and pragmatic thought processes within Practical Intellect. Ego psyche validates himself by means of percepts. Cognitive compensation occurs within mental operations as a psychological compromise within the interaction amongst earthly human system of reality, truth, and belief.

Cognitive confidence comes to exist within mental operations when cognitive awareness and intellectual evidence can overwhelm psyche awareness and perceptual evidence.

Cognitive deduction exists as a process of mental operations within logical thought by which thought (1) distinguishes relational schemata existing in Abstract Intellect as concepts of categorized and organized generalized common qualities and attributes of earthly reality, and, has been stored into memory, (2) abstracts the appropriate categories of relational schemata that might come to distinguish, define, and describe particulars of these generalized qualities and attributes relatively and idiosyncratically existing in observed objects, events, and others which are presently being sense experienced or sense perceived, (3) in order to cognitively discern that present sense experience and present sense perception can be validated by existing relational schemata, (4) then cognitively qualifying and quantifying the experience and the observation of presently existing objects, events, others by means of existing relational schemata, and, (5) transforming sense experienced and sense perceived information into Abstract Intellect as newly acquired knowledge.

Cognitive development exists as an extremely complex, intricate process of the possibility of the interaction and of the collaboration of many mental operations and many mental awarenesses. Cognitive development becomes dependent upon earthly human ability to acquire cognition and to feed that cognition with knowledge. Establishment of cognition relies upon processes of cognitive development, concept development, thought development, and language development, and learning. Human Mind Life establishes cognition, intellects, and ego psyche complimentary and stores knowledge. Learning requires concept development, thought development and language development, which cognitive functions in cognitive order to learn as inherent and intrinsic processes existing in human Mind Life toward developing cognition.

Cognitive development exists as the mentally operational process toward "realized" qualitative mental operations as the individual's relationship of conceptual development expands a conscious awareness of that knowledge of himself intellectually and psychologically interacting with earthly reality by means of sense experience through meaningful symbolic learning as process of both thought development and language development. Cognitive awareness transcendently transforms perceptual awareness as quality of cognition.

Cognitive development exists as an extremely complex, intricate process of the possibility of the interaction and of the collaboration of many mental operations and many mental awarenesses. Cognitive development becomes dependent upon earthly human ability to acquire cognition and to feed that cognition with knowledge. Establishment of cognition relies upon processes of cognitive development, concept development, thought development, and language development, and learning. Human Mind Life establishes cognition, intellects, and ego psyche, relationally, and, stores knowledge. Learning requires concept development, thought development and language development, which abilities to learn, are inherent and intrinsic processes existing in Human Mind Life toward developing cognition.

Cognitive disengagement occurs within ego psyche, when sense experience and sense perception, as well as perceptual evidence, cause ego psyche not be able to acquire psyche awareness. Ego psyche does not become aware of "self" as ego psyche, able "to recognize" that ego psyche acts as the facilitator and the qualifier between what earthly human body comes to sense experience as perception at a given time in a given space in a given reality, and, needs to become aware of possibility of "some" validation. Ego psyche disengages as much as possible from earthly reality.

Cognitive disequilibrium exists within mental operations when mental operations and knowledge cannot validate sense perception.

Cognitive dissatisfaction exists when mental operations cannot validate conscious awareness with knowledge with perceptual awareness with ego psyche within earthly reality.

Cognitive dissonance, existing within mental operations, exists as a mental void, when perceptual awareness supersedes intellectual awareness.

Cognitive emergence (egress) exists as a process of mental operations which permit an effecting or an affecting mentally deferential consequence upon sense experience and sense perception.

Cognitive equilibrium exists within mental operations when mental operations and knowledge can validate sense perception.

Cognitive induction, using logical definition of the term, might be (1) a cognitive process of evaluating the cognitive validity of a particular and immediate contextual and situational sense experience and of observation of earthly reality based upon the derived discernible common attributes of a class or genus, as inferential evidence toward validating a logical "a priori" proposition of general essence about all classes or genuses, or, (2) a form of logical reasoning that qualifies a conclusion apparently supported by sense experience and by observations of earthly reality although these external observations do not absolutely cognitively validate the conclusion, nevertheless, a cognitive "a priori" conclusion is drawn. Cognitive induction, using logical thought, attempts to cognitively validate into Abstract Intellect those particular, immediate sense experiences and sense perceptions by means of relational generalized schemata already existing "a priori" in Abstract Intellect.

Cognitive ingress exists as a process of mental operations which permit transformation of sense perception into existing knowledge.

Cognitive qualification exists as a status within mental operations when the mental operation of apprehension interacts with the mental operation of cognitive dissonance interacts with intellectual evidence. Sense experience provokes a sense perception of an earthly reality in a given time in a given contextual situation. Initially Practical Intellect forms a percept of that which has just been perceived of the contextual situational earthly reality. Cognitive qualification demands some intellectual validation of that "practical percept." Within an existing quality of cognitive development, thought development, concept development, and language development, if, these four mentally operational levels have not progressed beyond cognitive level of perceptual awareness, where mental operations remain at the level of ability to abstract primary concepts, then, ego psyche interacts either egocentrically, or, with lack of cognitive awareness. Cognitive development, thought development, and concept development have not moved Practical intellect beyond "conscious experience" of perceptual awareness. When Practical Intellect lacks sufficient cognitive awareness to abstract secondary concepts form practical Intellects force pro formed primary percepts of earthly reality, cognitive qualification becomes mental status of cognitive disequilibrium and cognitive dissatisfaction.

Cognitive reflection is a mental ability within mental operations which enables cognitive structure and cognitive functions to mentally consider their abilities and operations in cognitive order to achieve a cognitive resolution of intellectual validation. The mental ability of cognitive reflection requires the mental operations of analysis and synthesis. Analysis is the mental operational thought process which evokes the need for the deliberation (reflection and discernment) of cognitive ability within personal and idiosyncratic knowledge. Synthesis is the mental operational thought processes which cognitively orders cognitive ability with personal and idiosyncratic knowledge in cognitive order to achieve cognitive validation. Cognitive reflection exists as a cognitive function of cognitive awareness. Cognitive awareness exists as a cognitive function of conscious awareness. Qualitative conscious awareness demands qualitative cognitive awareness which both demand qualitative cognitive reflection when mental operations are attempting cognitive validation of that which ego psyche is sense experiencing and sense perceiving of relative, phenomenal earthly reality.

Cognitive resolution is a mental ability of a thought process within mental operations which requires a series of separate, defined thought processes: (1) analysis is the mental operational thought process which evokes the need for the deliberation of cognitive ability and personal and idiosyncratic knowledge; (2) reflection is a mental operational thought process which enables the use of cognitive ability and personal and idiosyncratic knowledge toward a consideration in an attempt to achieve a resolution of cognitive validation; (3) synthesis is the mental operational thought process which cognitively orders cognitive ability with personal and idiosyncratic knowledge in cognitive order to achieve cognitive validation; (4) transformation becomes the thinking process requiring the functions of all cognitive abilities, which include abstraction, cognitive awareness and the seven (7) mentally operational sub processes of cognitive awareness, as well as, the cognitive abilities of comprehension, understanding, and reasoning; transformation requires the use of Practical Intellect and Abstract Intellect; transformation requires thought and concept development; the mental operations occurring within the thought process of transformation result in the acquisition of new personal and idiosyncratic knowledge as well as newly acquired thought and concept development toward validation of the newly acquired knowledge with existing knowledge; transformation is the process of "transferring" one thought, existing as either precept or concept, into another thought, existing as either concept or percept; (5) conclusion is the mental operational thought process which enables a personal and idiosyncratic intellectual judgment to resolve cognitive validation. Cognitive resolution enables psychological resolution.

Cognitive responsibility exists as individual self-responsibility toward the personal and idiosyncratic development of cognitive structure and cognitive functions in mind as well as self-responsibility toward the acquisition of knowledge. Self-responsibility exists by virtue of ontological and epistemological authority to exist, as that notion of "inalienable right." Webster's definition of the word "inalienable" exist by "connotation" as "something absolute" that cannot be transferred. Webster's definition of the word "inalienable" exist by "denotation" as "something absolute" that can not be denied. If human holds existence, and, that ontological existence defines itself as inalienable, possessing rights of life, liberty, and happiness, then who or what, ontologically or epistemologically, becomes "responsible" for insuring the "inalienable rights." "Something uncertain called society, "something uncertain" called government, "something uncertain" called science, "something uncertain" called religion? If earthly human "right" exists as "inalienable," earthly human cannot transfer his "inalienable right" to "something other," because "absolute inalienable right" of earthly human cannot be "denied" by "something other," because "absolute" ontological and epistemological resolution that the "inalienable right" exists as the "self-responsibility" of earthly human remains inalienable to the earthly human. EVERY RIGHT ONTOLOGICALLY AND EPISTEMOLOGICALLY PRESUMES A RESPONSIBILITY! If in the case earthly human relinquishes his "responsibility" to a mandate of law, or, to a mandate of creed, or, to a theory of science, earthly human legally, morally, and ethically relinquishes his "right!" Human Nature, ontologically and epistemologically, everlastingly "keeps" responsibility for Human Nature inalienable right of self-responsibility.

Cognitive satisfaction exists when mental operations validate conscious awareness with knowledge with perceptual awareness with psyche with reality.

Cognitive validation exists within mental operations when intellect "a priori" realizes, by process of thinking within cognitive awareness and conscious conscious awareness, the transformation of sense perception of earthly reality into "metaphysically realized" absolute concepts of essence of existence within earthly reality.

Collective consciousness within contemporary population thinking has become synonymous with notion of social consciousness of secular humanism.

Collective unconsciousness, for Carl Jung, came to exist inherently, metaphysically over earthly time and earthly space within human ego psyche, as a personal consciousness or a personal unconsciousness, as a "representational realization" of the collective prototypical sublime pro formations of Human Nature existence. This collective unconsciousness, for Carl Jung, came to be "metaphysically realized representationally" as Prototypical Archetype essentials.

Commensurate exists when two "things" exist as the same "meaningful measure," or, to the same extent or to the same extant.

Common good becomes realized by virtue of the common will of reasonable earthly humans who enter freely and responsibly into social contract by means of rational consent.

Compelling force exists within mental operations as metaphysical quality needing validated linguistic and behavioral expression, validated by "a priori" innate knowledge. Compelling force exists as metaphysical quality of mental operations that brings forth attraction, fascination, inclination, allurement, mystery, inspiration, aspiration, appreciation, fulfillment as intellect interacts with ego psyche with earthly reality.

Compensation, within a status of mental operations, exists when cognitive awareness cannot validate perceptual awareness____abstract intellect cannot validate practical intellect____so practical intellect "transfers" invalidated sense perception to another invalidated sense perception in a mentally operational attempt to acquire some intellectual validation interacting by means of ego psyche. In the beginning____ in the cradle____a quality of compensational transference that exist at this time in earthly reality does not even have human body awareness of practical intellect, or perceptual awareness, or cognitive awareness. "Infant" mental operations, expressing attempt at compensational transference, exist at the psychophysiological level of sense experience whereby one sense perception is attempting validation with another sense perception____there exists no qualitative interaction between ego psyche and Abstract Intellect.

Compensational transference, within a status of mental operations, exists as a quality of mentally operational compensation when ego psyche attempts to transfer invalidated sense perception to another invalidated sense perception in attempt to pragmatically and practically qualify the invalidated sense experience within level of Practical Intellect.

Competent intellectual discernment about the nature of Practical or Abstract Intellect interacting with ego psyche interacting within earthly reality requires (1) sufficient facts (information) of the contextual and situational relative phenomenal earthly reality, (2) sufficient knowledge of the contextual and situational relative phenomenal earthly reality as compared to human Mind Life innate "a priori" knowledge of the success or failure of past earthly reality sense experiences of similar contextual and situational relative phenomenal earthly reality (3) sufficient knowledge of metaphysical prototypical archetypes of the essential nature of the concepts of an "ideal" earthly reality as opposed to only a perceived "in the moment" empirical earthly reality as possibility that conceptual comparative prototypes of earthly reality can validate this immediate perceived contextual and situational reality, (4) "worthy" conscience, and, (5) self responsibility of one's free will.

Complexity, existing within mental status, occurs when intellect's interaction with ego psyche cannot prevent ego psyche to continue to perceive multiple contextual and situational contradictions existing between two mental operations. Ego psyche is over-whelming intellects! Complexity verges into absurdity when intellects interacting with ego psyche cannot "conceive" the "perceiving" of ego psyche. Intellects cannot come to "conceive" a possibility of intellects coming to the aid and comfort of ego psyche interacting with earthly reality.

Comprehension cognitively develops in human Mind Life as the process of mental operations by which an human Mind Life ***begins*** mental processes of abstractly transcendentally transforming Practical Intellect primary percepts, existing as quality of earthly reality sense perceptions, sense impression, sense opinions (inferential intuitive guesses) into human Mind Life Abstract Intellect absolute universal secondary concepts.

The third mental operation (3) of cognitive development becomes the mental operation of *comprehension*. *Comprehension* of the meaningful relationship between Practical Intellect primary percepts and Abstract Intellect secondary concepts, abstractly transcendentally transforms primary percepts of earthly reality information into Abstract Intellect absolute universal secondary concepts by means of the mental operation of comprehending a cognitive deferential quality toward potential of "knowing something truthful." *Comprehension* is a mental operational structure and function of human Mind Life cognition, enabling the meaningful organizing and co-ordination of Practical Intellect with Abstract Intellect within a process of abstract conceptual thought interacting as language. After the abstracting mental operational process of comprehension, and, after the mental operations which occur within cognitive awareness, human Mind Life attempts to "make sense" of it all. These mental operational process of "making sense" of "sense perception" becomes the mentally operational state of comprehension by means of the use of secondary concepts. Comprehension "realizes" or "makes sense" from "sense perception" by means of intellectually validating by means of a cognitive resolution and a psychological resolution newly acquired knowledge with already validated "a priori" knowledge existing as personal and idiosyncratic systems of reality, systems of truth, and systems of belief toward the fourth mental operation (4) of cognitive development which is understanding.

Concept is a mental abstraction conditioned upon essence and existence of the mental operations of Human Nature essential existence of human Mind Life intellectual ability to mentally represent the classification, categorization, and organization of common critical attributes essential to the "knowing of" the possible qualities necessary toward the actuality of objects, events, and other beings____as well as Nature Nature and Human Nature. Metaphysical concepts are abstractly signified in human Mind Life in form of metaphysical conceptual language. Earthly reality empirical language has been established as an earthly reality consensual, socio-culturally shared sign system which designates socio-cultural symbolic (dictionary defined) meanings gearthly human senses experiencing earthly reality. Earthly reality established empirical language enables human Mind Life thought (as abstract idea) to come to acquire cognitive ability to force pro form in human Mind Life as abstractly metaphysically representing earthly reality empirical language information. Earthly reality empirical language holds two qualities (bestowed upon earthly reality empirical language by human Mind Life via cognitive processes). Earthly reality empirical language (1) holds empirical symbol representation (primary percepts), (2) which physical symbolic representation of physical earthly reality linguistic representation can transcendently transform physical information into abstract metaphysical essential meaning as a human Min Life concept.

Earthly reality is first sense experienced by earth human five senses. Ability of human Mind Life to abstract "spirit ideas" from earthly reality from sense experience and sense perception by human body substance has never been determined by science. Science prefers not to refer to "abstract concepts." Concepts may come to exist as primary concepts within human psychological Practical Intellect, or, with Abstract Intellect intelligent secondary concepts. Primary concepts exist within Practical Intellect as percepts. Primary concepts enable an immediate abstract impression of earthly reality forming primary percepts as perception, impression, or, opinion. Precarious, phenomenal Practical Intellect perceptions, impressions, opinions of earthly reality provoke human Mind Life need toward cognitive validation based upon Abstract Intellect intellectual evidence. Secondary concepts are "intellectually based." Secondary concepts "have been metaphysically realized" as a result of Abstract Intellect's ability to interact primary concepts (perceptions, impression, opinions of earthly reality) with "conceptual comparative prototypes" ("something absolutely known" beyond earthly reality physical. must interact with "anything uncertain" in physical earthly reality). Intellect, existing as abstract, conceptual thought, interacts with psychological ego psyche, ego psyche force pro forming as facilitator and mediator of possibility to come to cognitively, intellectually know earthly reality and Human Nature, as a conscience conscious awareness knowing, outside of the earthly reality physical, "trans spaces" relative phenomenal earthly reality establishing a conceptual, abstract absolute conscience conscious awareness of earthly reality.

Concept development, as it relates to cognitive development, is an individual's mental operational abstracting ability within human Mind Life acquisition of meaningfully validated primary and secondary concepts as processes of a ontogenetic, physiologically, phylogenetic evolution towards the sequential and orderly evolution of human Mind Life qualitative cognitive and psychological processes. The very nature of "humanness" (Human Nature) may be defined as maturational, cognitive processes of human Mind Life mental operations interacting force pro formed as earthly reality psychological quality of ego psyche interacting within a relative phenomenal earthly reality toward creating human Mind Life intelligence. The nature of humanness becomes a quality of human Mind Life manifesting human Mind Life within a relative phenomenal earthly reality as intelligence.

Conceptual awareness develops in both Practical Intellect and in Abstract Intellect. Conceptual awareness existing in Practical Intellect exists as a primary percept, which represents to human Mind Life a metaphysical quality of perception, impression, opinion of earthly reality based upon a biased relative phenomenal earthly reality. Primary percepts exist within Practical Intellect dependent upon (1) quality of environment, (2) quality of sense awareness, (3) quality of Practical Intellect, (4) quality of ego psyche awareness, (5) quality of perceptual awareness, and, (6) quality of personal awareness. Primary percepts come to exist in human Mind Life as earthly human personal and idiosyncratic perceptions, impressions, opinions of earthly reality. Perceptions, impressions, opinions of earthly reality exist as that status within mental operations, in which earthly human begins to acquire a sensual realization of objects, events, and other beings by means of the senses' observation of earthly reality stimuli, first, provoking the five senses, and then, provoking Practical Intellect ego psyche to mentally extrapolate a personal and idiosyncratic perception, impression, opinion in human Mind Life as earthly reality percept in human Mind Life. Perception, impression, opinion occurs as an immediate content and context reaction to situational and intentional stimuli offered by earthly reality. Perception, impression, opinion occurs as an initial reaction by psychological ego psyche attempting to facilitate a relationship between Practical Intellect and earthly reality. A mental perception, impression, opinion comes to exist as a percept____as a primary percept within Practical Intellect. Conceptual awareness existing in Abstract Intellect exists as a secondary concept, which represents to human Mind Life metaphysical unpredictable consequences of contradictions existing between that which Practical Intellect "knows" as earthly reality, and, that which Abstract Intellect "a priori knows" as metaphysical conceptual comparative prototypes of existence, actuality, and essence of existence. Abstract Intellect must resolve earthly reality unintended consequences caused by Practical Intellect ego psyche quality of earthly reality awareness.

Conceptual comparative prototypes exist innately in mind, as intellect, enabling human Mind Life to become the "constant absolute," existing as "the Absolute"'(essential categorical universals), in cognitive order to resolve intellectual conflict. Conceptual comparative prototypes resolve contradiction between that which psychological ego psyche perceives with that which Abstract Intellect stores as intellectual evidence using reason, however, not without earthly reality «physical unpredictable consequences.» Conceptual comparative prototypes exist "innately a priori" within Abstract Intellect metaphysically (beyond the physical). Abstract Intellect calls upon "innate a priori" sublime pro formational abstract concepts of the absolute Archetypes and Prototypes which define the essence of existence of Nature Nature, the universe, and, Human Nature. This "meaningful measure" intellectual evidence quality that "something absolute, "beyond the phenomenal physical realm, exists as "absolutely intellectual evidence quality as the "something absolute "that comes to validate anything earthly uncertain____to be able to come to know actual "should be nature" of essential existence. The "anything existing real" exists within earthly reality as quality of real, but not as quality of truth. "The clash" (cause)

of the metaphysical intellect with the metaphysical ego psyche result
as effects of "metaphysical unpredictable consequences" ____always in
earthly time and earthly space causing a new metaphysical/physical
conflict, contradictions, and, absurdities which require resolution by
intellectual evidence knowing the "absolute should be" Archetypes and
Prototype of the essence of existence.

Conceptualization exists within mental operations as a process of
cognitive structure and cognitive functions within both Practical
Intellect as a perceptual awareness and in Abstract Intellect as a
conscious awareness.

Concrete empirical stimulus, not so long ago, within earthly reality,
earthly reality thinking represented an abstract quality of earthly
reality earthly human established system of earthly reality, system of
truth, and system of belief in "how would an earthly human "socio-
cultural-political think" about earthly reality. Does earthly human
reason his "thinking" about his interaction with earthly reality? Does
an earthly human submit to any present socio-political thinking,
never asking why he submits? "Reason" quality of thinking about
earthly reality become identified in humankind histories as an ideal of
human ***Rationalism.*** Science said no! Earthly human only empirically
(earthly reality based holds no Mind Life ability to reason, there exists
no human Mind Life in Human Nature). Academics in United States
universities stretched earthly reality thinking "to believe" that earthly
human is incapable of reason because early human holds no Mind
Life, merely human body organism to react to earthly stimuli____Acts
of Speech that lack Acts of Knowledge. Presently, in contemporary
earthly reality, idea of Empiricism is winning over idea of Rationalism.
Contemporary earthly humans have been indoctrinated into ideas of
Empiricism____earthly human can come to know only by means of
earthly human physical body's physical substance of five senses; earthly
human holds no Mind Life, no free will, no soul____in contemporary
empirical fact____there is no god. This contemporary, (20th century),
empirical thinking society is the first humankind civilization to have
killed god! Contemporary earthly human has been indoctrinated into

contemporary socio-cultural-political empirical earthly reality thought based and biased upon the psychological ego psyches self-chosen elitist psychological ego psyche's self-centered attitudes. Contemporary self-centered elite earthly humans have been able to indoctrinate unconsciously aware earthly humans to believe their socio-cultural-political earthly reality thought. Without acknowledgment of earthly human metaphysical realm human Mind Life (Reason) earthly human exists merely as an earthly human organism capable of only following the Queen Bee (Political Elitist). Empiricism in contemporary earthly reality is winning; contemporary earthly reality killed god (human Mind Life reason).

Sense perception exists in human Mind Life as an abstract mental perception, impression, opinion of a earthly reality. Sense perception transforms sense experience into a primary concept placing the primary concept into Practical Intellect as a quality of an earthly percept. An earthly percept exists as an immediate perception, impression, opinion provoked by contextual, situational, empirical, concrete stimuli. Quality of percept depends upon quality of sense awareness and quality of self-centered ego psyche awareness. Percept comes to exist in quality of earthy reality practical and pragmatic Practical Intellect as quality of perception, impression, opinion. An earthly reality perception, impression, opinion becomes a mental image of a perceptual awareness effect, or, affect upon earthly reality as a percept as a result of sense experience and sense perception of immediate contextual situational earthly reality stimuli. Percepts build quality of human ego psyche. Percepts establish primary concepts into Practical Intellect. Primary concepts exist within Practical Intellect dependent upon (1) quality of environment, (2) quality of sense awareness, (3) quality of Practical Intellect, (4) quality of ego psyche awareness, and (5) quality of personal awareness. Primary concepts come to exist in Practical Intellect as quality of non-validated perceptions, impressions, opinions of earthly reality. Within contemporary earthly reality empirical thought, practical and pragmatic perceptions, impressions, opinions are winning over reason. Human ego psyche needs to meet human Mind Life.

Concrete-empirical stimuli (earthly reality) exists as "anything uncertain" "perceived as real," (while not necessarily true) that comes to provoke an earthly human behavior reaction____possibility of no human Mind Life foreknowledge, forethought, foresight into quality thought as forthright. Earthly human behavior as an action performed by human body substance, or, conventional usage of language expression comes to express an earthly reality quality of earthly human habit behavior, or, earthly human conventional habit language. Concrete-empirical stimuli, "perceived as real earthly reality" provokes an earthly human response____behavioral or linguistic interacting with earthly reality even if only as a sensible intuition guess. If it is mental property (brain) within human body substance that reacts and responds; empirical science suggests that earthly human body substance (as human organism) reaction or response, whether behavioral or linguistic, can be earthly reality observed, and, statistically measured by socially and psychologically earthly reality mathematical measure. "Meaningful measure" comes to be realized either in Practical Intellect or in Abstract Intellect when "some uncertain" measure of quantity of human sense experiences, or, of quantity of earthly human perceptions, or, of quantity of acquisition of earthly reality synthetic information does mysteriously tremendously transform earthly reality synthetic information into some quality earthly reality measure of quantity of earthly reality sense experiences, or, of quantity of earthly reality perceptions, or, of quantity of earthly reality synthetic information. Metaphysically cognitively, "meaningful measure" comes to be realized when "nothing earthly certain" "significantly," but, "suddenly" becomes "something realized as absolute," ____human Mind Life cognitively transformed earthly reality synthetic information uncertain into metaphysical understanding toward discovery of metaphysical absolutes existing in earthly reality synthetic uncertain information.

Within notion of "concrete-empirical stimuli" demanding an ***immediate*** earthly reality reaction or an ***immediate*** earthly reality response, the ***immediate*** reaction or the ***immediate*** response holds "no earthly quality of time" to consult with intellectual evidence as evidence of intelligent reaction or intelligent response which has been earthly reality recognized and realized as innately held "a priori" absolute quality of knowing innately "a priori" held in human Mind Life. Unless perception (ego psyche) interacts with Practical Intellect within *"immediate perceived"* relative earthly reality, the *immediate* ego psyche reaction or response will be compromised by the status of quality of earthly reality uncertain synthetic information presented as concrete-empirical earthly reality quality of uncertain synthetic informational stimuli. As an *immediate* reaction or *immediate* response to earthly reality concrete-empirical stimuli non-validated earthly reality synthetically uncertain information, possessing no intellectual evidence quality of thoughtful resolution, no quality of social ideological evaluation, or, no long turn psychological satisfaction has had no "time to think, to reflect, to discern, or, to free will human Mind Life contemplation toward discernment of absolute truth.

"Meaningful measure" results in a "matterfilled consequence," a perceptual decision void of "meaningful measure" of responsible intellectually evident worthy consequence. Result as earthly reality "matterfilled consequence" suddenly, but non-significantly becoming "nothing" becoming "nothing." (Jean-Paul Sartre, **Being and Nothingness**).

Conditioned behaviors come to exist as a result of conditioned behavioral response, habit, imitation, indoctrination, dominant population thinking. Conditioned behaviors may result as intended or unintended consequences from extrinsic earthly reality uncertain synthetic informational influences, or, may result as intended consequences from intrinsically thought-out discernment and human Mind Life free will to think metaphysical thought.

Congruency comes to exist as a quality status within mental operations when perceptual evidence and perceptual awareness have acquired enough perceptual confidence to make a perceptual judgment about that which Practical Intellect has sense perceived from a sense experience in psychological order to coalesce perception of a contextual, situational reality by validating the perception with "a priori" intellectual evidence existing in Abstract Intellect. Congruency within mental operations becomes significant to enable memory to store "a priori" intellectual evidence necessary to validate new sense perception of new sense experiences in earthly time in earthly space in earthly reality seeking cognitive and intellectual congruency with earthly reality sense perception as earthly reality quality of synthetic "a posteriori" knowing cognitively validated by human Mind Life absolute "a priori" knowing.

Connotes is a mentally operational ability to translate thought into language, either as suggested or as specified, as word meaning attempting to enter the suggested or specified word meaning into contextual and situational sense experience and sense perception in attempt at mutual communication.

Conscience, as a mental operation, exists as a mental propensity toward cognitive confidence of a need to discern right from wrong____ metaphysical human Mind Life concept of right or wrong is not always consciencely "meaningful measured" within earthly reality sense experiences. Ignorance as stupidity and intelligence as intellectual evidence becomes "meaningful measure" of right or wrong. Mental state of conscience may exist as a mentally operational propensity toward realizing the cognitive ability of reason. Mental state of conscience moves toward cognitive confidence of the possibility of recognizing right from wrong____as intelligence versus stupidity. When mental operations fail to validate perceptual awareness with cognitive awareness with conscience conscious awareness in matterfilled confidence of metaphysical awareness of concept of "right from wrong" conscience, or, intelligence, gets involved. Mentally operational status of cognitive disequilibrium and psychological disequilibrium will come to exist in "con-science" when sense perception cannot validate with conscious awareness mental operation of conscience, or, intelligence____ evoking cognitive and psychological dissatisfaction. Cognitive and psychological dissatisfaction results because sense experience and sense perception of the observation of "evil" behavior cannot become perceptually validated by human Mind Life conscience awareness of intelligent conscious awareness. Ego psyche psychologically self-centeredly tells

Practical Intellect that this ego psyche "self unsatisfying behavior is evil." Ego psyche refuses "to listen to Abstract Intellect," psychologically disavowing ego psyche of self-responsibility to use human Mind Life intellectual evidence in cognitive order to attempt conscience conscious awareness validation of "evil," or, ignorant earthly reality behavior. Metaphysical Abstract Intellect, existing within mentally operational status of conscience, "knows innately a priori" the conceptual comparative prototypes that define, within Abstract Intellect, the difference between right and wrong___between intelligent and stupid earthly reality behavior. Psychological ego psyche compensational transference relies upon perceptual multiple observations of "evil" behaviors as justification for "another perceptual observation of evil behavior." One "evil" behavior does not justify another "evil" behavior. One misguided behavior does not come to validate another misguided behavior. "Everyone does it" does not come to justify "misguided behavior."

Conscious experience equals perceptual evidence which exists as an imbalance amongst intellectual awareness with personal awareness with psychological awareness with perceptual awareness with ego psyche awareness within earthly reality. Perceptual evidence exists in Practical Intellect as conscious experience of perceptual evidence of sense experience and sense perception.

Conscious awareness exists within mental operations as a mental ability which permits earthly reality to become mentally, cognitively aware of his personal and idiosyncratic knowledge and cognitive structures using cognitive functions of perceptual awareness, abstraction (or conceptualization), cognitive awareness, comprehension, understanding, and reasoning. Perception comes to exist as earthly reality empirically stimulated thought, while conceptualization is autonomous and spontaneous metaphysical cognitive thought. Conscious awareness realizes the mental operations occurring within both Practical Intellect and Abstract Intellect. Without conscious awareness no cognitive metaphysical thought could occur, no transformation from Practical Intellect primary concepts into Abstract Intellect secondary concepts could occur. Conscious awareness exists as a perceptual awareness during the mental operational processes of earthly reality physical realm directed sense stimulation, perceptual observation, immediate mental impression occurring within Practical Intellect interacting as psychological ego psyche with earthly reality. Human conscious awareness seeks human Mind Life conscience conscious awareness.

Conscious awareness comes to exist as a learned, acquired cognitive awareness during the mental operational processes occurring as metaphysical cognitive functions within Abstract Intellect interacting with earthly reality. Conscious awareness integrates the perceptual mental processes of Practical Intellect with the conceptual metaphysical Abstract Intellect by means of cognitive reflection, analysis, synthesis, discernment, cognitive mental operational judgment, and human free will within the process of thinking transforming perceptual awareness into intellectual awareness. Conscious awareness encompasses self-consciousness, personal awareness, intellectual awareness, cognitive awareness, psychological awareness, ego psyche awareness, perceptual practical awareness, and conscience. Conscious awareness exists as the interconnectedness amongst intellects, ego psyche, with earthly reality.

Consequences, intended or unintended, result from quality of perceptual evidence within Practical Intellect, or, result from quality of intellectual evidence within Abstract Intellect manifested in earthly reality as either language or behavior.

Contemplation becomes a process of mental operations within thought development, concept development, and Abstract Intellect moving towards "possibility of actuality." Contemplation, for Plotinus, existed within mental operations as a metaphysical realization of human Mind Life cognitive level of reason. When human Mind Life enters into cognitive quality of mental operation of reason, human Mind Life enters into a status of contemplation. Mental operational status of contemplation releases human Mind Life from "metaphysical unpredictable consequences."

Contemporary exists within the same earthly time within a sociocentric earthly reality of earthly humans. In this manuscript contemporary time period is present day.

Content exists as subject-oriented information expressed via language or behavior isolated within any given earthly reality situation in earthly reality time in earthly reality space in earthly reality.

Context exists as subject-oriented heresy information expressed via language or behavior isolated within a specific and particular situation in a given time in a given space in earthly reality.

Contingent, within mental operations, may become a process of thinking that becomes dependent upon a previous sense perception of a previous sense experience to validate a new sense perception of new sense experience in social order to make a perceptual decision within a given context within a given situation within a given earthly reality, or, may become a process of metaphysical awareness that choses to consciously aware refer to intellectual evidence existing within Abstract Intellect in cognitive order to resolve contradiction, conflict, absurdity as ego psyche judgment as ego psyche interacts with earthly reality.

Contradiction comes to manifest itself within mental operations when intellects attempt to cognitively resolve incongruity or inconsistency between what Abstract Intellect "conceives" about earthly reality and what Practical Intellect "perceives" about earthly reality. Contradiction comes to manifest itself within Practical and Abstract Intellects when Abstract Intellect cannot cognitively validate conflicting "ideas" existing within intellectual evidence due to Practical Intellects synthetic uncertain sense perceptions. Contradiction exists within Practical Intellect as synthetic, non-intellectually validated sense percepts, and, in Abstract Intellect as metaphysical concepts when Practical Intellect and Abstract Intellect cannot validate each other. A mental operational status of incommensurability comes to exist as mental operations have no common basis of an absolute criterial standard of comparison. Contradictions, within mental operations, result when intellectual evidence within Abstract Intellect cannot cognitively validate perceptual evidence within Practical Intellect when human ego psyche, too earthly reality dependent, cannot cognitively qualify human ego psyche's sense perception of sense experience as actual conscious awareness held innately "a priori" in Abstract Intellect.

Construal exist as a sociological term referring to the notion that earthly humans use subjective perceptions as a means of relating to earthly reality. The mental operation of construal becomes an empirical perception without any intellectual evidence bases within Abstract Intellect metaphysical awareness of earthly reality. Construal becomes that phenomena of earthly reality phenomenal perceptions by which earthly human uses "second-hand" earthly reality synthetic information in social order to "make a non-qualitatively, cognitively involved judgment call" (1) due to lack of direct experience with contextual situations, and, (2) due to lack of intellect's sufficient knowledge, or, lack within intellectual acumen, to "make a qualitatively, cognitively involved judgment call."

Critical knowledge comes to exist within mental operations as process of critical thought of earthly reality phenomenal sense perceptions, sense impressions, and sense opinions of earthly reality____none of which speak truth. Intellectual knowledge innately "a priori" held in human Mind Life does not attempt criticism in cognitive order to validate truth of phenomenal perceptions, impressions, opinions of earthly reality. Human Mind Life uses intellectual evidence in cognitive order as attempt to demonstrate that earthly human sense perceptions, sense impressions, and sense opinions are not intellectual truth. Earthly reality criticism holds no earthly reality metaphysically aware meaning or value.

Critical Theory exists as a system of reality, system of truth, and a system of belief that "society" can be "changed" by "critiquing" it.... then... developing and proposing a "social scientific paradigm" to "fix" society. Whereas philosophical speculation attempts to reasonably discern humankind's relationship with Nature Nature and Human Nature. The Frankfurt School presented itself as a notion proffering "socially-oriented thought" based as "a critique of society." This manuscript suggests that the Frankfurt School, (1898-1975), made up of a collaboration of sociology professors and politically-minded socialist, were attempting to discern just "how a society could come to know a secular socialistic society?!" The Frankfurt School established what they called a Critical Theory attempting to discern (1) what reason should socially mean, (2) an analysis of the conditions necessary toward social emancipation and social desalination, and, (3) a critique of modern capitalism. The Frankfurt School of thought was attempting to use a neo-Marxism dialectical approach toward resolving the social contradictions existing within modern capitalist society. Critical Theory Ideology critiquing capitalism existing as a free market economy existing within earthly reality only caused earthly human social and economic inequality and exploitation of the worker. In consideration that "Critical Theory" might develop "critical thought" might develop "critical knowledge" of "true" relationship between earthly human and earthy reality, whereby critical analysis becomes earthly reality dependent upon set group perceptions, impression, opinions of the inequalities presented by Capitalism. Critical Theory might critically resolve economic system of capitalism that causes social inequality and elimination of set group desalination by introduction of ideology of Socialism.

Speculative philosophy of Hegel suggested that relationship between earthly human and earthly reality presented earthly human Mind Life with "constant contradiction." Human Mind Life "constant contradiction" between Practical Intellect and Abstract Intellect did not exist due to physical realm society. Human Mind Life "constant contradiction" came to exist due to earthly human synthetic, invalidated sense perceptions, sense impressions, sense opinions of society____earthly human sense perceptions, sense impressions, sense opinions of earthly reality did not mentally operationally coalesce with human Mind Life innate "a priori' "should be" conscious awareness conception of earthly human existing in "should' be" earthly reality. Hegel's Objective Mind was always in conflict with Subjective Mind, and, Hegel suggested a cognitive method of ***resolving cognitive conflict***___dialectical reasoning using recognized and realized innate "a priori" human Mind Life knowledge.

"Constant contradiction," existing within earthly reality, results from *"cognitive conflict"* existing within human Mind Life. Earthly human sense perceptions of earthly reality do not cognitively intellectually coalesce with absolute metaphysical concepts innately existing "a priori" in human Mind Life___resulting in human Mind Life cognitive conflict. Human Mind Life cognitive mental operations attempt to resolve cognitive conflict. Human Mind Life does not intellectually validate the worthiness of concept of criticism; human Mind Life intelligently seeks truth.

Society can only be as "productively and positively critical" of itself, as Hegel suggested, by reasonable virtue of the meaningful measure of human Mind Life metaphysical awareness of essential existence. Any society's ability to "knowledgeably conceptually reason" to resolve contradiction depended upon the ability to reason by Everyman member of the society. "Knowledgeably conceptual reason" requires mentally operational use of Abstract Intellect's metaphysical realization of comparative conceptual prototypes of the essence of existence in cognitive order to validate or to invalidate sense perceptions of earthly reality. Where does earthly human discover truth?

Critical thought comes to exist within mental operations when intellectual contradictions presented to Abstract Intellect by Practical Intellect cannot coalesce with innately known "a priori" metaphysical awareness of Nature Nature, universe, and Human Nature. Earthly reality, existing phenomenally without truth, cannot validate earthly reality "a posteriori" perceptions, impressions, and opinions of earthly reality as truth. Human Mind Life innate "a priori" knowledge of absolute truth demands mental operations to validate or to invalidate that which Practical Intellect, existing as psychological quality of human ego psyche, merely sense perceives earthly reality. Everyman sense perceives earthly reality differently from Everyman. Where does Anyman discover truth in earthly reality? Critical thought brings forth dialectical reasoning. Dialectic (Hegelian dialectic) suggested that a mentally operational interpretative method might be possible as means toward theoretical resolve amongst opposing or contradictory earthly reality perceptions with human Mind Life conceptions of earthly reality. One proposition (thesis or hypothesis) has become identified as contradictory to another proposition (anti-thesis or hypothesis). The cognitive, intellectual goal is to resolve earthly reality synthetic contradictory propositions into one agreed upon "thesis proposition." Hegel did not seek a "synthesis; a "synthesis," for Hegel, meant "a mutual agreement;" Hegel did not seek a "mutual agreement." Hegel sought an "absolute idea" by means of a "higher" level of realized metaphysical awareness forming "a theoretical whole" of the contradictory perceptions coalesced with human Mind Life innate "a priori" conceptions. For Hegel, the "dialectical moment" coming to exist within metaphysical awareness in human Mind Life as metaphysical awareness of an earthly reality existing so relatively uncertain could only exist as continual temporary "mental moments" of synthetic thesis propositions. In cognitive social order there has to come to exist temporary "mental moments" of agreeable "should be" cognitive thesis propositions. "Theoretical" thought, for Hegel, only presented more speculative "theory" (synthetic hypothesis). In cognitive order for a "true" dialectical discussion to come to resolve "incommensurability" within earthly reality contradictory interpretations, resolve must appear as renewed "self-conscious" awareness within conscious awareness____ continual conscious awareness of renewed, enhanced, enriched knowledge! Dialectical reasoning continued as long as Subjective Mind was beholding to Objective Mind, and, as long as Objective Mind was beholding to Subjective Mind!

Within contemporary society **critical thought** has socio-cultural-politically developed into criticism, skepticism, condemnation, censure, impossibility of earthly human to earthly human profound learned reconciliation. Contemporary earthly human must learn to think positively!

DNA symbolizes deoxyribonucleic acid as the name of a molecule that enables genetic mapping as physiological development and function of living organisms.

Data is a collection of earthly reality synthetic information which earthly reality information awaits transcendental transformation into human Mind Life knowledge in cognitive order to become cognitively intellectually comprehended and cognitively intellectually understood in cognitive order to ever be considered as possibility of the acknowledgment of "truth." Earthly reality information must be cognitively intellectually transformed into cognitive intellectual knowledge by cognitive structure and cognitive functions in Human Mind Life in cognitive order to be acknowledged as personally comprehended and understood conscious awareness of earthly reality synthetic information as intellectual truth____not just status of uncertain precariously perceived earthly synthetic information.

Decision exists as a quality of mental operations within cognitive intellectual deliberation, discernment, cognitive judgment, or, merely a status of uncertain, never validated as truth perceptual judgment.

Deconstruction was a notion of language analysis toward possibility of meaningful interpretation presented by the French philosopher Jacques Derrida (1930-2004). Language comes to be a conventionally agreed upon, accepted, and used sign and symbol (semiotic) system written and spoken within a syntactical form. Meaningful interpretation of language by means of reading and hearing language required "deconstruction" of the "semantics" of language, according to Derrida. "How a word comes to mean," according to Derrida, was made possible by virtue of the nature of language usage. Language presented human Mind Life with the necessity toward meaningful, valuable intellectual interpretation. According to Derrida, because the nature of language demanded meaningful, valuable, intellectual interpretation, language also presented human Mind Life with contradictions demanding resolution due to the multitudes word meanings that were bestowed upon language by earthly human set group perceptions of earthly reality. According to Derrida, language presented to human Mind Life recognizable "play of differences." These "differences" both "signed" and "signified" to human Mind Life the necessary contingency of "conscious awareness" of "hierarchical differences in meaning itself" (more significant or less significant value of metaphysical meanings.). "Difference" is the systematic play of differences of hierarchal levels of cognitive metaphysical meanings, which essential meanings must become cognitively, validly related to each other within cognitive order. For example: in discussion regarding right of individual liberty and social necessity of common safety for all individuals, which of the two metaphysical concepts have prior hierarchy? For example: in political behavior expression, which of the two metaphysical concepts have prior hierarchy ___political power over the behavioral destruction, defamation, ridicule of a human being.

According to Derrida, "la differance" calls up (demands) "mental moments of mental spacing" as a temporization, a detour, or, a postponement by means of which sense perception, earthly reality quality sensible intuition, socio-cultural-political consummation_____ via set group meaning of the word, contemporary ideological socio-cultural-political propensity, present circumstantial situation give greater hierarchal meaning to the meaning of the word than does human Mind Life innate "a priori" metaphysical awareness of absolute truth, decency, integrity, honor, trust, kind, good?

Language comprehension and interpretation brings into play a certain not conscious experience calculation. Derrida's necessary contingency of cognitive understanding toward human Mind Life innate sublime pro formational Logos (absolute word meaning) demands human Mind Life conscious awareness of the intelligent nature of Human Nature. For Derrida, language held two essential attributes___in earthly reality language meant any Everyman's ego psyche wishfully desired meaning; in human Mind Life metaphysical language held only absolute meaning.

Defense mechanism comes to exist both linguistically and behaviorally provoked by psychological human ego psyche not referring to human

Mind Life intellectual evidence. Defense mechanism comes to be manifested in earthly reality as cognitive compensation, psychological compensation, and compensational transference_____one invalidated perception to another invalidated perception void of any intellectual evidence.

Deliberation is a mental ability existing within mental operations as a capability of cognitive intellectual discernment. Deliberation becomes cognitive process of the capability of the mental operation of cognitive intellectual discernment. Deliberation, within mental operations, occurs as a provocation by Practical Intellect using perceptual evidence in social order to make a perceptual decision; or, occurs as a quality cognitive capability of Abstract Intellect using intellectual evidence in cognitive order to make an intelligently discerned judgment toward intended or unintended consequences.

Demiurge is a concept, originating within Plato's philosophy, of the possibility of "a creator," or, "mythical artificer," who was "the responsible one" who "artfully" fashioned the "real," if only "perceptible" world as well as any possible "conception" of the "ideals" of that world. In Gnostic philosophy the demiurge exists as "a duality of good and evil" suggesting that the material universe displays itself as evil, while, the non-material human Mind Life innate "a priori" ideals possess qualities of possible goodness.

Denotes is a mentally operational ability to translate thought into language in which words signify a specified word dictionary meaning in an attempt at mutual communication within contextual and situational experience.

Deportment exists as a manifestation or expression of "self" toward "others." Deportment may manifest or express the conveyance of "an aura" of intellectual and psychological self-confidence as a self-awareness. Deportment may manifest or express the conveyance of a certain false pretense.

Derrida's Differences. According to Jacques Derrida, (1930-2004), because the nature of language demanded meaningful interpretation, language also presented human Mind Life with cognitive contradictions demanding cognitive resolution. According to Derrida, language presented to human Mind Life recognizable "play of differences." Language meaning "differences" both "signed" and "signified" to human Mind Life cognitive conscious awareness of meaningful and valuable hierarchical differences (more significant or less significant). "La differance" comes to cognitively exist in human Mind Life as a schematic systematic play of differences demanding "mental moments" of mentally operational epicycle spacing by means of which cognitive schemas must become cognitively, validly related to each other. "La differance" calls up (demands) that cognitive mental operational epicycle spacing as a temporization, a detour, or a postponement by means of which perception, earthly reality sensible intuition, socio-cultural-political consummation____via cognitive deliberation search innate "a priori" knowledge toward discernment of truth. Cognitive relationship to an earthly reality present, cognitive reference to an earthly reality present reality, to an earthly reality present existence must be deferred until cognitively validated. Comprehensively deferred by virtue of the very principle of "la differences" which demand human Mind Life cognitive functions to validate "a posteriori" earthly reality contextual, situational word significance to human Mind Life innate "a priori" metaphysically aware significance. Cognitive economic aspect of "la differance," brings "into play a certain not conscious experience calculation" (Derrida's notion of earthly reality word significance to human Mind Life metaphysical significance within cognitive mentally operational force pro formance which demand reference inseparable from the mere semiotic aspect (the mere sign) to human Mind Life "la differance" of that which human Mind Life innately "a priori" knows" that the "sign" (word), within earthly reality comes temporarily, at a moment in earthly reality time, to temporarily mean. (wiki, Deconstruction).

Determinative existed as a language symbol during ancient times when language was in the form of pictograms or hieroglyphics. A determinative, a symbol in cognitive order to avoid any disambiguation, was attached to the writings in cognitive order to attempt the significant meaning desired from the writing.

Disambiguation, within cognitive thought, results due to cognitive inability to reconcile existing Practical Intellect percept of earthly reality with an immediate, contextual, and situational newly sense experienced Practical Intellect percept. Disambiguation occurs within mental operations due to cognitive inability to reconcile concept with percept. Disambiguation occurs when intended meanings in language do not cognitively relay due to differing earthly human differing perceptions, impressions, opinions, under discussion of topic, contextually and situationally existing earthly reality "a posteriori" perpetual opposed to human Mind Life "a priori" conceptual.

Discernment becomes a capability within mental operations to integrate the mental operations of cognitive awareness (and the seven cognitive functions of cognitive awareness), the mental operation of comprehension, and, the mental operation of understanding of that which has been sense perceived by means of sense experience. Discernment attempts quality cognitive meaning from earthly reality synthetic information coalescing intellectual evidence with psychological awareness in cognitive order to place value and meaning upon earthly reality synthetic information in cognitive validation using human Mind Life intellectual evidence. Quality of psychological determination, quality of intellectual evidence, quality of use of cognitive structure and cognitive functions greatly assist intellectual discernment, otherwise, result as no occurrence of intellectual discernment.

Disengagement occurs within ego psyche, when sense experience and sense perception, as well as perceptual evidence, cause ego psyche not to be able to acquire ego psyche awareness. Ego psyche does not become aware of "self" as ego psyche, able "to recognize" that ego psyche acts as the facilitator and the qualifier between that which human body substance comes to sense experience as sense perception of earthly reality at a given time in a given space in a given earthly reality, sense experiences need to be validated by intellectual awareness of cognitive intellectual validation. Ego psyche psychologically selfishly disengages as much as possible from Abstract Intellect interacting with earthly reality choosing to remain in earthly reality status of psychologically selfishly pleasuring ego psyche.

Disposition exists in earthly human as acquired habitual tendency to behave and to speak as the earthly human ego psyche has acquired selfish or unselfish self awareness.

Dynamic exists as status of mental operations as a continuous force pro formance of Practical Intellect alongside Abstract Intellect toward mental operational ability as motivation toward cognitive and intellectual development which may come to effect and to affect stability within cognitive and psychological equilibrium as well as cognitive and psychological satisfaction.

Earthly-centered exists as earthly-centered linguistic terminology void of any and all human Mind Life metaphysical language, or, metaphysical awareness. Earthly-centered linguistic terminology is earthly reality spoken as earthly-centered human body substance sense experiences of earthly reality____as sense perception, sense impression, sense opinion sense experiences of earthly reality socio-cultural-political physical realm____voided of any and all human Mind Life intellectual evidence. As example: establishing a system of metaphysical belief is not the same as establishing an earthly-centered system of opinions. Opinion holds bases and bias in sense experience of earthly reality current dominant physical status quo. System of belief demands human Mind Life contemplation, discernment, abstract quality of cognitive comprehension and abstract quality of cognitive understanding beyond earthly reality physical reality of human body substance sense experiences. Earthly-centered perceptions, impressions, opinions use earthly-catered perceptions, impressions, opinions tin social order to speak that which earthly human has and is sense experiencing____voided of any and all human Mind Life intellectual cognitive discernment.

Effecting exists as an ability of mental operations able to influence a non-emotional consequence.

Enigma exists as a puzzling, ambiguous, inexplicable social awareness.

Ego psyche, existing in earthly reality as earthly human ego psyche, as earthly-centered and self-centered psychological and perceptual ego psyche personality and self persona, earthly-centeredly and self-centeredly psychologically interacts with other earthly human psychological earthly-centered, self-centered ego psyches, personalities, and personas within an earthly-centered and self-centered earthly reality gamesmanship distinguished by Charles Darwin called "survival of the fittest." Earthly human hereditary genotypes, and, earthly human environmental phenotypes are modern science's explanation of Charles Darwin's "survival of the fittest."

Egocentric thought exists as a quality within mental operations by which earthly human validates system of reality by means of his egocentrism; viewing earthly reality in relation to himself biased upon a system of secular contemporary belief that the world exists, or can be known, only in relation to his psychological ego psyche interacting with earthly reality acquired social, political, and materially synthetic information. Egocentrism may be discussed as either a philosophical or a psychological possibility of a quality of human Practical Intellect.

Elitism exists as a notion that there exists in time in space in earthly reality a set group of earthly humans sharing common system of reality, system of truth, and system of belief who have been able to overwhelm contemporary dominant population thinking by their personal and idiosyncratic system of reality, system of truth, and system of belief biased within their own egocentric and sociocentric ego psyche awareness of a secular sociocentric ideology.

Emotion exists as a quality within mental operations by means of which earthly human discerns the value of the organizational cognitive ordering of the acquisition of any new knowledge validated with existing knowledge toward a possibility of acquiring a personal and idiosyncratic system of reality, system of truth, and system of belief. Emotion may have a positive or non-positive effecting or affecting influence upon mental operations and their consequences as emotion interacts with quality of ego psyche awareness. Quality of ego psyche is influenced by quality of emotion because emotion functions as both an intellectual and a psychologically influencing mental qualifier between intellects and ego psyche interacting within earthly reality. Emotion has nothing to do with "feeling;" feeling resides within the sense experience of touch, whereas the cognitive function of emotion resides within human Mind Life mental operations. Emotion as a mentally operational qualifier will influence cognitive satisfaction, cognitive dissatisfaction, cognitive equilibrium, cognitive disequilibrium, psychological resolution, psychological satisfaction.

Empirical exists as concrete physical earthly reality of sense experienced earthly reality which comes to be known by means of sense perception of sense experience. Empirical earthly reality denies any metaphysical potential quality to earthly human existence. Empirical real exists as as an empirical real human body substance sense experience.

Empiricism is a theory that proposes that human knowledge can be acquired only by means of sense experience and sense perception. Empiricism, existing as theory, suggests the human Mind Life can come to inductively consciously experience knowledge gained by means of sense experience and sense perception of observable earthly reality as sense perceptual evidence that earthly reality is real. Empiricism, existing as a theory, suggests that by using scientific method in the establishment of hypotheses of theories that must be tested by observation, experimentation, and data collecting of a world that really exists, even within a relative phenomenal earthly reality, will come to acquire conscious experience of the real natural world. Empiricism, existing as theory, ***denies*** (1) human Mind Life ability "to reason" "a priori" by means of some innately mentally operational "a priori" prototypical "ideals," (2) that human Mind Life innately exists as mental operations "to think," which mental operations supposedly interact metaphysically between human Mind Life and earthly reality, (3) that there exist a soul and ego psyche, (4) that human Mind Life innately holds intellectual potential, (5) that human Mind Life can become potentially intellectually "enlightened" (6) that there exist notion of an collective unconsciousness that inherently comes to "realize" itself within human Mind Life as metaphysical conceptual prototypical exemplars of an "intelligently designed" Nature Nature, universe, Human Nature.

Engagement exists within mental operations as a mental operational process by which earthly human uses the mental operation of cognitive resolution in cognitive order to validate perceptual awareness with existing Human Mind Life innate "a priori" knowledge awareness.

Environment biophysically surrounds earthly human existing within earthly reality. Environment requires earthly human to biophysically adapt, culturally advance, cognitively develop, and, to acquire knowledge of Nature Nature and Human Nature in cognitive order to intelligently interact with earthly reality environment as Human Nature potential to do so. Environment encompasses both natural phenomena and earthly reality phenomena.

Environmental determinism exists as a scientific notion that climate, geography, natural resources, environmental diseases come to set physical limits upon human environmental earthly reality. Contemporary system of belief in science has taken this notion to the extreme that earthly human metaphysical Mind Life holds no intellectual ability to control earthly human environment. Therefore it becomes the obligation of contemporary system of belief in science, social scientific paradigms, and governmental ideologies to attempt to control earthly human behaviors within earthly reality environment. This becomes the answer to the question "who are they," when media reports that "they say." "They" are contemporary science, contemporary social science, aided and abetted by a few bad, ugly, ignorant earthly humans.

Essence exists by ontological nature and teleological purpose by virtue of human, animal, or inorganic substance to exist as that meaning and significance, that mystery, that sacredness, that profundity of its essential existence and its essential actuality.

EVOLUTIONARY PSYCHOLOGY proposed that earthly human substance mental property brain operates as an adapting mechanism much like the evolutionary physiology of earthly human physical body substance _____as human psychological need to evolve (physically adapt) in earthly reality order to survive. Evolutionary psychological addresses the notion that earthly human body substance organ brain was comprised of multiple functional physiological mechanisms each existing as specific domain modules... such as language acquisition module, parental investing module, sexual trait modules____over earthly reality time physiologically evolving within human body physical substance organ brain sense experiences within socio-cultural behaviors. Since human body substance organ brain is a computational physiological human body substance mechanism, earthly human physical organ brain can physiologically compute "input" of new sense experience by means of "representing" (science has not yet figured out just how; nor was the great human Mind Life of Renee Descartes)) new sense experience with appropriate existing modules in earthly reality survival order to physiologically "output" a corresponding sense response by means of human body substance five senses. Socio-cultural conditions greatly influence facultative adaptations, which asked the question "if-then." Evolutionary psychologists concern themselves with how environmental "inputs" produce earthly human propensity toward establishing relationships such as in marriage or parenting as evolved earthly reality physiological "output." Evolutionary psychologists contend that acquired socio-cultural behaviors that become universally accepted and manifested within a dominant culture can be considered as evolutionary adaptations toward becoming new situational earthly reality environments. Nevertheless, scientific theory of evolutionary psychological ***does*** adhere to "some" physiological possibility that human body substance organ brain also holds "mental" property.

Existence manifests existence as a reality that reality exists, by and of itself... by virtue of its existence because human body physical and mental substances can "really" sense experience existence____naming "what existence is" becomes a mysterious conundrum.

Expression exists as a metaphysical quality of mental operations because mental operations in human Mind Life innately need pronouncement within linguistic elucidation and within behavioral manifestation. Quality of expression depends upon quality of Practical Intellect interacting with quality of Abstract Intellect interacting with personal and idiosyncratic metaphysical knowledge. Expression exists both linguistically and behaviorally. Expression may rely only upon perception, perceptual awareness, perceptual evidence within Practical Intellect, and, due to ego psyche expression of free will may not interact with mental operations within Abstract Intellect which rely upon intellectual evidence. Ego psyche expression may chose perceptual evidence permitting ego psyche to overwhelm Abstract Intellect. Ego psyche expression performs an act of speech as an act of regurgitating earthly reality synthetic information, or, behaving an act of perceptual decision within a given time, within a given space, within a given earthly reality without cognitive awareness of unintended consequences. Cognitive expression may chose intellectual evidence in cognitive order to allow an act of knowledge to force pro form intellectual evidence linguistic expression, or, force pro form behavior as intellectual discernment expression. Expression exists as a metaphysical quality within metaphysical mental operations because metaphysical mental operations innately need pronouncement within linguistic elucidation and within self-responsible behavioral manifestation. Quality of earthly reality expression depends upon quality of Practical Intellect interacting with quality of Abstract Intellect interacting with personal metaphysical knowledge awareness. Practical Intellect expresses Practical Intellect earthly reality practical and pragmatically. Practical Intellect relies upon earthly reality perceptual awareness, ego psyche awareness, psychological emotion, and dominant socio-political culture thinking.

Faith exists as Human Nature mentally operational ability to acquire metaphysical cognitive confidence within necessarily contingent principles as essential attributes meaningful and valuable toward accepting a system of belief upon faith in necessarily contingent principles metaphysically realized. Necessary continent attributes of the realization of the existence of humanness becomes the realization of an essence of the existence of humanness.

Faith, existing as mental status of conscience cognitive confidence, establishes Human Nature earthly reality system of earthly reality, a system of truth, and a system of belief in the essence of the existence of humanness. Cognitive confidence accepting a system of belief has been established within a quality of conscience cognitive awareness of a quality of conscious awareness of essence of humanness. Conscience cognitive awareness of quality of conscious awareness of essence of humanness, an earthly human maintains faith in his system of reality, system of truth, and system of belief, otherwise, an early human would go insane. Establishing and accepting a system of belief upon faith, existing as conscience cognitive confidence in metaphysically realized necessary contingent human essence does not require psychological resolution or psychological qualification because mentally operational ability of faith has no psychological confidence in ego psyche relationship with earthly reality when ego psyche has no interaction with metaphysical conscience conscious awareness. Conscience cognitive mentally operational ability of faith maintains an earthly human system of belief. An earthly human conscience cognitively validates his system of belief within human Mind Life innate "a priori" knowledge____innate "a priori" knowledge capable of supporting intellectual evidence that places both value on and reason for earthly existence. Faith in human Mind Life innate "a priori" knowledge force pro forms earthly human system of faith regardless of cognitive measure of quantity and of quality of human Mind Life "a posteriori" knowledge, or, the quality of his cognitive awareness of his conscious awareness. Due to "meaningful measure" of quality of innate "a priori" knowledge force pro forming within human Mind Life cognitive awareness, human Mind Life conscience conscious awareness holds faith in Human Nature. Human Mind Life Abstract Intellect will chose to place in abeyance perceptual decisions made about earthly reality until human ego psyche psychological awareness can integrate personal awareness, intellectual awareness, and conscience conscious awareness toward faith in Human Nature.

Why does there exist within earthly reality moral and civil transgressions? Plato told because of earthly human non-awareness of intelligently designed Human Nature____never metaphysically cognitively intelligently recognized and realized.

Faith existing in practical intellect may establish a system of faith into a system of belief enabling a faith-valued intellectual confidence toward the practice of a defined or undefined religious creed. Faith existing in practical intellect may establish a system of faith into a system of belief enabling cognitive and psychological confidence within the praxis of an established, participatory conscience aware social order. (As example, money has no value *existing merely as a piece of paper*, but, that piece of paper, authorized by a government, as "money," gains its assigned value as faith-valued by the participating earthly humans). Earthly human "choses" to acquire faith as quality of practical intellect as an earthly reality support system that earthly human is not insane. Faith, existing as a system of faith, may come to establish psychological and perceptual confidence, into a system of reality, a system of truth, and a system of belief, void of cognitive confidence, psychological confidence, and intellectual evidence. If an earthly human possess no intellectual evidence "by virtue of the reason why" earthly human willfully participates in social praxis, whether existing as religion, or, as government, or, as society, the only cognitive ability that affords earthly human aid and comfort for human "existence," becomes based in earthly human's "faith" in his system of reality, system of truth, and system of belief.

Final cause exists as philosophic, metaphysical idea historically credited to Aristotle's philosophic speculation of Teleology suggesting that there exists "final cause" in Nature Nature and in Hunan Nature____ both Nature and Human Nature have in intended, intelligent purpose. Human Mind Life innate "a priori" knowledge provokes earthly human to ask "why!" Infant human Mind Life, just out of the cradle, starts to ask "why!' Intrinsic "final cause why" exists "by virtue of reason that Human Nature earthly exists surrounded by Nature Nature." Extrinsic "final cause why" exists "by virtue of reason to exist toward significant effect." Notion of teleology was first suggested by Aristotle, (384b.c.-322b.c.), further speculated by Anselm of Canterbury, (1033-1109), and, Immanuel Kant, (1724-18040, and, Georg Wilhelm Friedrich Hegel, (1770-1831). The difference between Teleonomy and Teleology reside in thought within two different worldviews. Teleonomy resides within scientific theory; while Teleology resides within philosophic speculation. Metaphysical conceptual thought speculates that "final cause" "gives significance of purpose for earthly existence." Teleonomy suggests that genotypes and phenotypes give "biological, physiological" determination to human organism as "human final cause" for existence "non-randomly" selected by virtue of biological physiological happenstance, **yet randomly**, selected because no two earthly humans will ever possess the same DNA ___scientifically determined not necessary toward a "final cause," rather physiologically, biologically toward the continuance of infinite energy. Humanness existing in earthly reality is merely a temporary state of infinite energy. Teleology suggests there is more to human existence than genotypes and phenotypes. Teleology suggests that human Mind Life and human free will determine earthly human quality of earthly existence toward an intelligent, intended purpose. There is more. Teleology suggests that earthly human existence holds an essential "final cause." Both Greek philosophy and Enlightenment philosophy attempted speculation as to "what is" human final cause.

In defense of metaphysics, Richard Feynman, (1918-1988), an American physicist, made certain statements during Feynman's scientific studies perhaps not intentionally stated "in defense of metaphysics," however, the scientific observations of natural scientists, such as Max Planck and Albert Einstein, do not permit them to ignore metaphysical thought ignorantly only offering favor to science. Here is presented to the reader some of the quotes offered by Richard Feynman___

"We scientist are clever—-too clever—-are you satisfied? Is four square miles in one bomb not enough? Men are still thinking. Just tell us how big you want it?"

"In the age of specialization men who thoroughly know one field are often incompetent to discuss another. The great problems of the relations between one and another aspect of human activity have been discussed less and less in public. When we look at the past great debates on these subject we feel jealous of those times, for we should have liked the excitement of such argument. The old problems, such as the relation between science and religion, are still with us, and I believe present as difficult dilemmas as ever, but they are not often publicly discussed because of the limitations of specialization. (Author's note: politicians behave their entire adult life behaving politics____politics is all they know. Followers of politicians behave their lives as followers of their favored politics____never questioning or discussing why____politics rules their lives).

"How can we stand together to support these two pillars of Western Civilization (science and religion)? Is this not the central problem of our time?" (Paraphrased)

"The real problem in speech is not precise language. The problem is clear language."

"A great deal more truth can become known than can be proven."

"Science is the belief in the ignorance of the experts."

Finalism suggests notion of teleology. Notion of teleology was proposed by Plato and Aristotle, by Saint Anselm in the 11th century AD, and later, by Immanuel Kant, Georg Wilhelm Friedrich Hegel, and Carl Jung. "Anything earthly uncertain "has extrinsic finality because it is only essentially contingent within an immediate contextual situation. The immediate contextual situation occurs randomly and accidentally without any Teleonomy predetermination, or, intellectual forethought. "Anything earthly uncertain" has intrinsic finality when it exisst by virtue of its reason to exist even though the "anything earthly uncertain" did not always exist and will not always exist. Plato, Aristotle, and Aquinas suggested that the human body substance has extrinsic finality because it will cease to exist; the human soul has intrinsic finality because the human soul will not cease to exist because the human soul's finality becomes the realization of its teleological purpose to exist... its final perfection. Immanuel Kant, Georg Wilhelm Friedrich Hegel, and Carl Jung suggested that while it is that Human Intelligence, Knowledge, Spirit, Self may be temporarily encapsulated within a physical body, Human Intelligence, Knowledge, Spirit, Self teleologically develop toward a final perfection which *is* by virtue of the reason Human Nature essentially exists. Jean-Baptiste Lamarck suggested that even within scientific notion of evolution, epigenetic influences propel human toward a final perfection. Charles Darwin suggested that within scientific notion of evolution no two humans will ever be genetically the same. Ernst Mayr's notion of perfection was that human body, as a physiological organism, naturally selects to adapt as perfectly as possible earthly human interaction with earthly reality regardless of "positive or negative" environmental influences. Ernst Mayr suggested that one of earthly human evolution is the humans' striving toward perfection whether physiologically or intellectually.

First philosophy, according to Aristotle, is metaphysics.

First principles, according to Aristotle, are universal essential principles, (natures, sources, prototypes), whose actualities of possibilities cannot be reduced further.

Five senses exist as physical property within human body substance interacting with each other as well as physiologically and neurologically interacting with physical organ brain. The five senses of human body substance stimulate metaphysical human Mind Life to acquire knowledge of earthly reality, and, enable metaphysical human Mind Life to use language expression and behavioral manifestation by earthly human in earthly reality. The five senses are sight, hearing, smell, taste, and touch. Speech is not one of the five senses; speech requires metaphysical thought, otherwise, void of metaphysical thought human body substance can emit only sounds.

Force pro formance actuates ***Sublime pro formations*** which exist innately "a priori" in human Mind Life. Sublime pro formations exist as absolute, necessary, universal, and everlastingly true. Sublime pro formations define Human Nature. Human Nature exists absolutely necessary, and, universally everlastingly once an earthly human has been created as Intelligent Design. Human Nature exists sublimely pro formed absolutely to Human Nature essence. Human nature essence exists as the universal everlasting absolute archetypes and prototypes that define Human Nature____truth, equal, fair, trust, honor, rectitude, probity, good, moral, reasonable. Human Nature is Human Nature, otherwise, Human Nature is not Human Nature_____any earthly existence not true to itself does not exist as itself as earthly reality ***actual*** existence.

Foreknowledge brings forth foresight, forethought, and forthright within mental operations. Human Nature is defined by metaphysical concepts of truth (foreknowledge). Water is always water—-matter is always matter—energy is always energy____intelligent Human Nature is always intelligent Human Nature. Earthly reality and psychological ego psyche corrupt. Human Nature comes with "a priori" innate foreknowledge which enables earthly human Mind Life to recognize and to realize metaphysical knowledge of Human Nature as Human Nature essential existence. Within earthy reality process of learning human Mind Life "a posteriori" is provoke to recognize and to realize by meaning seeking Abstract Intellect a coalesce of earthly reality "a posteriori' sense experience (earthly reality learning) with "a priori' innate knowledge of foreknowledge absolute truths which combined bring forth into earthly reality a Human Nature.

Foreknowledge brings forth foresight, forethought, and forthright within mental operations. Foreknowledge comes to exist as the intellectual ability that has coalesced "a priori" innate knowledge which earthly human comes with, with "a priori" knowledge which earthly human acquires as a process of learning, with the "a posteriori" knowledge earthy human acquires from the sense perceptions of sense experience as earthly human lives earthly life "in temporia" in earthly time and space, within the fourth cognitive developmental level of the understanding and the fifth cognitive developmental level of reason bringing forth "fore" knowledge coming to exist as depth and breath of "meaningful measure" of intellectual evidence.

Foreknowledge brings forth foresight, forethought, and forthright within mental operations. Foreknowledge comes to exist as the intellectual ability that has coalesced human Mind Life "a priori" innate knowledge which is Human Nature, with synthetic "a posteriori" knowledge which earthly human acquires as a process of cognitive learning. Via cognitive learning human Mind Life enhances conscious awareness of ecumenical knowledge.

Foresight brings forth forethought using foreknowledge, existing within the mental operations of the fourth cognitive developmental level of understanding and the fifth cognitive developmental level of reason bringing forth a depth and breath of "meaningful measure" of intellectual evidence, coming to exist as **foresight,** occurring **previous** to any behavioral reaction that may be stimulated by sense perception of sense experience.

Forethought brings forth foresight using foreknowledge, existing within the mental operations of the fourth cognitive developmental level of understanding and the fifth cognitive developmental level of reason bringing forth a depth and breath of "meaningful measure" of intellectual evidence, coming to exist as intellectual foreknowledge, using comprehensive foresight (intellectual intuition) to cognitively use intellectual foresight previous to any earthly reality behavioral reaction that may be stimulated by uncertain, unvalidated perceptions, impressions, opinions human body substance interacting with phenomenal earthly reality psychologically invoked in human body substance body pleasure to satisfy idly prideful ego psyche.

Human Mind Life quality of cognitively acquired *forethought* becomes quality of intellectual intuition____a cognitive immediate process of human Mind Life to recognize and to realize cognitive understanding of earthly reality sense experiences as "meaningful measure."

Forethought exists within mental operations as the ability to mediate innate "a priori" knowledge innately forced pro formed as "a priori" in cognitive order to enrich, to enhance renewed knowledge in Human Mind Life intellectually recognized and realized from sense experience "a posteriori" sense experiences with earthly reality.

"Forms" exist as Plato's philosophic speculation upon "how it is that earthly human comes to know."

For Plato "Forms" existed as the prototypical, essential categories of existence, that actuality of Human Nature essence of existence as necessary metaphysically conceptual comparative prototypes toward the realization of the existence, actuality, and essence of existence which Practical Intellect falsely "seemed" to perceive in earthly reality. For Plato these "Forms" existed innate to human Mind Life, otherwise, without force pro formed innate knowledge that absolutely defined Human Nature "earthly human existing in earthly reality would never come to know!" The "Forms" were Plato's philosophic explanation of "how earthly human comes to know."

Formal cause exists as a notion that the **formal cause** of "something" is the by virtue of the reason the "something" exists as the "something."

Forthright comes to exist within the mental operations of cognitive understanding and of cognitive reason when human Mind Life intellect has acquired sufficient sagacious intellectual evidence in cognitive order to process language expression and behavioral manifestation with cognitive confidence.

Freedom exists within mental operations as an abstract archetypical idea (concept). Freedom has potential to manifest ideal freedom within earthly reality when earthly human in a society acquires conscious awareness of human Mind Life cognitive awareness, human Mind Life intellectual evidence, Human Nature free will, and Human Nature self-responsibility.

Free will exists as a quality of mental operations taking self-responsibility for intentions of their resolutions toward contradictions existing between Practical Intellect (perceptual evidence) and Abstract Intellect (intellectual evidence).

Genotype is a scientific assessment of biology, heredity human physiological gene description in scientific order to attempt to determine hereditary within human species evolution. Genes are inherited as the result of copulation between a male organism and a female organism passed onto their progeny. Mutation, genetic drift, pathogens, distinction, variation, in inherited human genes has not yet been able to be determined by either biology or genetics. Charles Darwin and Ernst Mayr both suggested that no two humans will ever have the same genetic makeup.

Ghost in the Machine is a notion presented by Gilbert Ryle, (1900-1976), suggesting that traditional religion or traditional theoretical thought or philosophic speculation may have presumed that there existed "a human mind" within body substance, and, Ryle suggested that presented man with a notion that there was a "Ghost in the Machine!" Gilbert Ryle, (1900-1976, **The Concept of Mind**), suggested that not only was there no "Ghost in the Machine," there was no human mind within body substance.

Good comes to exist within mental operations when earthly human has faith that his system of reality, his system of truth, and his system of belief will never cause harm to himself or to another. Perception lives pragmatical attempting to force "what is" into that which "should be." Good brings forth the forthright____the belief in a system of reality and in a system of truth that would never bring forth harm to self, or, to another, or, to the world. Concept of ***good*** requires metaphysical awareness to develop cognitively and to acquire knowledge, and, demands ego psyche to never speak lacking polite learning.

Good Faith comes to exist within mental operations when an individual has faith that his system of reality, his system of truth, and his system of belief will never cause harm to himself or to another.

Habit can be advantageous or disadvantageous; habits become repetitive learned cognitive behaviors; quality of a habit depends upon quality of cognitive structure and cognitive functions as well as quality of life experience. A quality of cognitive structure and cognitive functions as well as a quality of behavioral experience has a possibility of becoming good habit.

Hearing exists as one of the five senses as physical property within human body substance. The sense of hearing physiologically and neurologically stimulates a metaphysical awareness to force pro form conscious awareness of cognitive awareness, concept development, thought development, language development, psychological development, and the acquisition of knowledge.

Hermeneutics is earthly human interpretive method toward acquiring a system of reality, a system of truth, and a system of belief. Hermeneutics is earthly human interpretive method of earthly reality information which might be discerned either by means of a quality of Practical Intellect limited to ego psyche awareness and perceptual awareness, or, which might be discerned by means of the use of "a priori" knowledge and by means of a quality of personal and idiosyncratic intellectual evidence. Hermeneutics that attempts intellectual interpretation of religious text as truth still remains interpretation of one person's system of reality, system of truth, and system of belief, as Biblical or Talmudic story telling attempting to be interpreted by another's personal and idiosyncratic intellectual evidence____at best in good faith. Another intellectual limitation presents itself within use of various languages which need to be translated____text lost in translation. Use of language in social order to transform thought, even within the same language, remains based and biased within earthly human level of cognitive development, level of concept development, level of language development, quality of acquired knowledge, and quality of ego psyche awareness. Hermeneutics presents to earthly reality informational conundrum. Hermeneutical interpretation quality present to earthly reality an arbitrariness of perceptual awareness quality of Practical Intellect. Hermetical interpretation uses conventional language system which opens language interpretation to multitudes of earthly reality informational perceptions, impressions, and opinions. Hermeneutics can only be interpretation based and biased within philosophical speculation, an assuage of religious creed, that which history tells, or, a biased story telling of that which historicism retells. Each earthly human must read, read, read different biased points of view in cognitive order to acquire his own personal, but, nevertheless, idiosyncratic system of reality, system of truth, and system of belief.

History exists as an academic study of humankind's past events, advancements, wins and defeats. Philosophy of history speculates upon the ontological nature (reason for) and the teleological purpose of earthly human existence within phenomena of earthly reality history. History tells; historicism retells by means of hermeneutics.

Historicism, as a story telling of humankind past history, exists no more or no less than any other "ism."

"ism" is a suffix added to the end of a noun or a verb which connotes, as well as denotes, the measure of an "abstract" quality to the original connotation or denotation of language noun or verb... by the addition of the suffix "ism" physical language noun or verb acquires an "abstract" quality of becoming a universally recognized theoretical "ideology." The etymology of the suffix "ism" originated with ancient Greek connotative and denotative terminology in cognitive order to give meaning to a human Mind Life idea as now becoming recognized acquiring abstract force pro formance of an "abstract" quality within intellectual understanding. Historicism exists as an "ism," an abstract theoretically "story telling" that comes to gain theoretical value in the form of "an ideology." The story teller of Historicism uses human Mind Life cognition personal and idiosyncratic system of reality, system of truth, and system of belief in cognitive order to retell history by means of an interpretive story. Georg Wilhelm Friedrich Hegel, in his book, **The Philosophy of History,** interpreted humankind history by means of philosophic speculation, not by means of establishing an ideology, rather hoping to resolve contradictions amongst ideologies. Karl Marx interpreted humankind history by means of historical materialism, and, Marx's historicism brought forth an ideology. Anthropology, theories of human evolution, as well as contemporary social scientific paradigms use contextual interpretive historicism in social order to place theoretical value to their views of humankind history. Notion of human evolution has become a modern ideology. Social scientific paradigms have come to establish neither epistemologically nor theoretical quality of thought, but, rather forms of contemporary ideology, as examples, secularism and socialism. Thomas Kuhn, (1922-1996), suggested that within social scientific paradigms the use of historicism tends to lack epistemological commensurability. Historicism is a form of hermeneutics, and, like hermeneutics, historicists must rely upon earthly human personal and idiosyncratic systems of reality, systems of truth, and systems of belief. Myth, religion, social sciences, anthropology, theories of evolution, history provide earthly human with earthly reality information for genre of interpretive historicism. Jacques Lacan, (1901-1981), Michael Foucault, (1926-1984), Jurgen Habermas, (1929-), were not and are not historicists per se, they were and are critical theorists, which might be considered as the contemporary notion of historicism. Can hermeneutics, historicism, or critical thinking bring forth cognitive "meaning measure" of a quality of human Mind Life cognitive understanding as cognitive understanding meaningful measure of human Mind Life cognitive understanding, sufficient and significant enough to cognitively "meaningfully measure" past humankind history to humankind present behaviors and language? Is it that "a mere measure" of knowledge can bring forth "an ecumenical meaningful measure" of human Mind Life level of cognitive understanding? How is it that "a measure" of knowledge is to be "measured?" By personal and idiosyncratic interpretation, by personal and idiosyncratic perspective, by personal and idiosyncratic critical thinking? What ever happened to philosophic speculative "meaningful measure" of epistemology?

Homeostasis, as existing within relationship between earthly human and earthly reality, even while existing phenomenally dynamically, attempts stable equilibrium between earthly human interacting with earthly reality. Self existing physiologically, self existing psychologically, and self existing as intelligence interacting with other intellects in cognitive order to attempt to maintain socio-cultural and political stability and harmony could result in homeostasis. Science as "discovery" has come to respect the homeostasis already existing within Nature Nature order. Contemporary social science, as well as, industries involved in food production, either attempt to by pass the natural order, or, attempt to alter it. Any possibility of interpersonal interaction manifesting homeostasis requires "high" levels of intellectual acumen and psychological adeptness, as well as, "a fair share of kindness." When kindness fails, there becomes morality, when morality fails there becomes ethics, when ethics fails there becomes religion, when religion fails there becomes government, when government fails____there is only kindness.

Homo Sapiens Sapient exists as an anthropological term classification of a hierarchical taxonomy of the genus species of the modern anatomical earthly human. The term "homo" originates from the Latin word "homo." Carl Linnaeus, (1707-1778), coined the term "Homo Sapiens Sapient," even though Linnaeus, as a botanist, was more concerned with "behavioral" characteristics than with forming cognitive and epistemological perspective upon "how it is that human might be considered wise!" The word sapient connotes cognitive and epistemological characteristic or quality of being "wise!" In his book, <u>Systema Naturae,</u> Linnaeus points out that both species, human and monkey, have basically the same anatomy, monkey and human are "manlike." The only difference being that human has acquired "communicable?" language. Carl Linnaeus stated that he seeks a generic difference between man and the simian that can be based upon the principles of Natural History. Linnaeus stated: "I absolutely know of none. If only someone would tell me a single one." Linnaeus feared the wrath of creeds and principles of theology when Linnaeus made such an observation of man. Natural History of man assumes a chain of anatomical genesis of the animal species. However, even contemporary discipline of genetics has shown that genetic markers existing within modern human and present ape or present chimpanzee are similar. What is it that distinguishes modern earthly human from the animal, or, modern earthly human from his species of Hominid, Homo, or Homo Sapiens ancestors? Theology suggests that it is the "spiritual" quality of the human soul that distinguishes human from the animal soul. What is that distinction between the human soul and the animal soul? Linnaeus had suggested that the distinction was "that human learns to know Human Mind Life. Theories of evolution got it wrong. It is not language that brought forth a hierarchical distinction of human from human sub-species... it is human Mind Life intellectual potentiality toward acquiring unlimited knowledge, as cognitive quality level of the understanding, that distinguishes Human Sapient from even Human UnSapient____forget any comparison with animal sub-species. Conventional language cannot even communicate human Mind Life commensurate metaphysical, or, earthly reality information amongst earthly humans.

Humanness, whether it remains a phenomena of the evolution of species, or, a phenomena of a species adaptation to environment, or a phenomena of a qualitative process of intellectual design, humanness, as an existence in time in space in earthly reality, has not been adequately defined, not by evolutionary theories, anthropology, psychology, the social sciences, biology, or genetics. Attempt at explaining Humanness has been philosophically and theologically speculated. Carl Jung has probably been the only psychoanalyst to attempt such a fete.

Human-Reality connection. For Jacques Derrida, (1930-2004), language could transform the "transcendentally essential" into the "transcendentally empirical" at the same time in the same space in earthly reality that language could transform the "transcendentally empirical" into the "transcendentally essential. "Language could enable transcendental thought to relate by means of mentally operational comprehension, rational meaning held within human Mind Life thought, using an empirical, conventional language. In cognitive order to "conceive" language usage as "transcending" (trans spacing) empirical earthly reality, human Mind Life needed to recognize and to realize that empirical language only functioned as "signing"(assigning) as a "signifier" of that which was already held transcendentally "a priori" within human Mind Life. This was Derrida's explanation of Descartes' human-reality connection.

Human thought. There are four styles of thinking: (1) thought based upon theory, scientific theory or philosophical speculation (2) thought based upon faith and belief, (3) thought acquired by means of perception, and, (4) thought acquired by means of realizing concepts.

Idea may come to exist as a perception within Practical Intellect, or, as a concept within Abstract Intellect.

Idealism exists as a system of belief that each individual can bring forth, by intellect and by behavior, a "worthy" system of reality, system of truth, an system of belief.

Ideology might come to exist within mental operations as conscious or unconscious Ideals of human existence coming to establish personal and idiosyncratic system of reality, system of truth, and system of belief. Ideology might come to form sentient behavioral attractions, and/or, metaphysical attractiveness coming to be expressed in language as dominant population thinking, or, coming to be manifested in revolutionary behaviors.

Idiosyncratic thought exists as a quality within mental operations which becomes unique to each earthly human. Idiosyncratic thought remains personal unable to be transferred to another earthly human ability to cognitively comprehend.

Illocutionary speech act, within linguistic expression, denotes a quality of emotive speaking used to express the speaker's motivation towards effecting and affecting an immediate intended impression. Illocutionary speech acts may emote expression denoting assertiveness, directive, commitment, declaration, all within an intonation of "forceful" verbal, emotive expression. Once upon a time illocutionary performance in speech was regarded as a art form of rhetoric that could possibly aesthetically nourish human Mind Life.

Imagination exists as a quality within mental operations which enables cognitive structure and cognitive functions to collaboratively co-ordinate emotionally valued knowledge which has been stored in memory with a motivation toward new conscious awareness as well as new cognitively structured thought with a possibility toward mentally creative use.

Imitation, within mental operations, presents itself as consideration both linguistically and behaviorally. Primordial hominid and homo may have initiated human behaviors such as survival, adaptation to environment, and work. Contemporary human behavior as well as language expression imitates population thinking. as a Greek philosophical notion of "mimesis," which becomes the dialectical imitation of any current population thinking. Plato suggested the any "form" of imitation only can represent the "Forms" innately held in human Mind Life, otherwise, imitation reflects the meme of the predominate perceptions "a fortiori" of the current population thinking.

Immanuel Kant, (1724-1804), first proposed notions of analytic a priori propositions, synthetic a posteriori propositions, and synthetic a priori propositions in his <u>Critique</u> <u>of</u> <u>Pure</u> <u>Reason</u>. Kant argued that intellectual awareness of analytic a priori propositions supported notion of possibility of metaphysical concepts. Abstract mathematical propositions, Kant labeled as "analytic a priori" because mathematical statements provoked knowledge which could not be garnered by means of sense experience, "propositional mathematical knowledge" required some measure of the abstract "transcendental quality of understanding," not dependent upon sense experience or sense perception. Abstract mathematical concepts, existing "analytic a priori" required "first principle" metaphysical concepts residing within "a priori intellect" as "conceptual a priori" knowledge, which may have originally been provoked by sense experience, however, had needed to become cognitively understood without aid of sense experience, and, placed conceptually into memory into intellect. These abstractly realized mathematical concepts could then enable intellect, via logical thought existing as cognitive processes, "to analyze" any newly sense experienced "a posteriori" mathematical propositions toward validation by means of cognitive processes existing innately "a priori" in intellect, and, by means of mathematical knowledge existing "conceptually a priori" in intellect. "Synthetic a posteriori" propositions came to provoke acquisition of knowledge by sense experience and sense perception, however, remained as "synthetic a posteriori" information until validated by already existing "a priori" knowledge. "Synthetic a posteriori" propositions enabled acquisition of knowledge by means of sense experience and sense perception, and, remained "synthetic a posteriori" until they were transformed into new "a priori" knowledge. "Synthetic a priori" propositions came to exist as "transformational thought." "Synthetic a priori" thoughts (propositions) existed as those "thoughts" awaiting intellectual validation, and, remained "synthetic a priori" until they were acquired as new "a priori" knowledge.

Immutability comes to exist within mental operations when acts of knowledge become physiologically and perceptually unchangeable. Morality, reason, goodness, kindness are immutable.

Impression exists as a mental effect, affect, or a mental image retained in human Mind Life as a mental percept as the result of sense experience and sense perception. An impression opens itself to interpretation and to repudiation.

Inclusion exists as the result of mental operational processes occurring within (1) practical intellect when a perception, after "inferential inductive repudiation," can become acknowledged by means of "substantive deduction" occurring within (2) abstract intellect in cognitive order to transform a percept into a concept.

Incommensurability exists within mental operations as mental status when two or more percepts or concepts cannot come to validate each other by means of basis of commonality as standard of comparison, whether as having empirical value or epistemological value. Contradiction exists within practical intellect as percepts or in abstract intellect as concepts when mental operations come to deny or cannot validate percepts with percepts with concepts. A mental operational status of incommensurability comes to exist when mental operations have no common basis of standard of comparison. Earthly human existing in earthly reality hold no standard of comparison in social order to commensurate earthly human perceptions, impressions, opinions as possibility of cognitive comprehension and cognitive understanding.

Incompetence comes to exist within mental operations when there does not exist sufficient quality of knowledge to make a competent intellectual discernment about the nature of intellects interacting with ego psyche interacting within earthly reality. Competent intellectual discernment about the nature of intellects interacting with ego psyche interacting within earthly reality requires (1) sufficient earthly reality social facts (information) of the contextual and situational phenomenal earthly reality, (2) sufficient knowledge of the contextual and situational phenomenal earthly reality as compared to individual personal and idiosyncratic "a priori" knowledge of the success or failure of past experiences of similar contextual and situational phenomenal earthly realities, (3) sufficient knowledge of metaphysical prototypical archetypes of the essential nature of the concepts of an "ideal" metaphysical realm as opposed to only a perceived "in the moment" empirical earthly reality as possibility that conceptual comparative prototypes, archetypes, absolutes, universals can validate merely perceived contextual and situational phenomenal earthly reality, (4) "worthy" conscience, and, (5) self responsibility of human Mind Life free will.

Incompetence conspiring with intention comes to exist when there does not exist sufficient quality knowledge to make a competent intellectual discernment within cognitive mental operations therefore mental operations, usually existing within quality of practical intellect, compensate by allowing ego psyche awareness and perceptual awareness to bring forth a perceptual decision. Competence interacting with intention willfully bring forth self-responsibility toward the consequence. Incompetence conspiring with intention compensate for lack of will to take self-responsibility for the consequence.

Incremental becomes a quality within mental operations by which mental acquisitions become greater over time in space in reality.

Indirect speech acts, as proposed by John Searle, (1932-**The Construction of Social Reality**), are intentional thoughts using an illocutionary speech act in order to convey the specific intention of the speaker to the listener(s) without using language which may explicitly express the intention. The intentional meaning of the thought is "intentionally" masked by word usage, but, nevertheless, the intention of the meaning is comprehended by the listener(s).

Indirect speech acts, as proposed by John Searle, (1932-), are intentional thoughts using an illocutionary speech act in social order to convey the specific intention of the speaker to the listener(s) without using language which may explicitly express the intention. The intentional meaning of the thought is "intentionally" masked by word usage, and, the intention of the language used, as well as, how language is used is not comprehended by the listener(s) as the speaker's intentions, rather the Acts of Speech force pro form perceptions, impressions, opinions of the speaker.

Individuation, according to Carl Jung, become an individual's ability to use conscious awareness of intellectual and personal awareness in cognitive order to integrate psychological awareness in "self" formation of personality as a "coherent whole." For Jung, apart from maintaining physical health, achieving a qualitative conscious awareness and a positive psychological awareness enabled an individual to acquire "harmonious" and "mature" integration of personality within a system of values that inherently cognitively understood Human Nature and Nature Nature. Individuation, for Jung, enabled an individually realized integration of ego psyche with a qualitative completeness of all mental states of awareness.... with no mental or psychological dependence upon "anyone" or "anything" existing outside of the individual.

Indoctrination becomes that process of using earthly reality socio-political information in social order to stimulate socio-political thought towards particular theories or ideologies. Indoctrination exists as that quality of mental operations in which earthly human acquires perceptual awareness of events, objects, and other beings as the result of the directed instruction or exposure to a specific system of belief.

Induction, using logical inductive definition of the term, might be (1) a cognitive process of evaluating the cognitive validity of sense experience and of observation of reality based upon the derived, discernible common attributes of a class or genus, as evidence toward formulating a logical proposition of general rule about all classes or genuses, or, (2) a form of logical inductive reasoning that qualifies a conclusion apparently supported by sense experience and by the observations of the reality, although these observations do not absolutely cognitively validate the conclusion, nevertheless, cause a conclusion to be drawn.

Inductive inference, within mental operations, exists as inductive thought (induction) in order to infer a logical and reasonable conclusion using cognitive processes to evaluate and to validate sense perception of sense experience using argument, discussion, observation, however, not necessarily capable to achieve apodictic certainty or ampliative conclusion.

Inference exists as a mental quality of cognitive function by which earthly human affects a mentally operational conclusion from argument, discussion, or observation, which conclusion, awaits cognitive validation, or, remains as an "a posteriori" earthly life experience, not necessarily achieving apodictic certainty or ampliative conclusion.

Inferential evidence exists within mental operations after the mentally operational process of inference has arrived at a mentally operational conclusion from argument, discussion, observation, which conclusion, may not necessarily have achieved apodictic certainty or ampliative conclusion, but, nevertheless, perceptually arrived at evidence (percept) that will continue to be used as inferential evidence.

Information and Knowledge are not the same thing. Earthly reality information exists as empirical data transmitted and received via earthly reality language____as epistemological quality of earthly reality contextual, situational information "in the moment." Earthly reality information exists as public data based within the bias and the perception, the impressions, and the opinions of that media which transmits that earthly reality information. Knowledge and Information are not the same thing. Earthly reality information can be cognitively transcendently transformed into conscious aware idiosyncratic and personal knowledge. Earthly reality information exists as physical language written as squiggles on the page, or, spoken as sounds heard. Earthly reality information does potentially possess for the human Mind Life acquiring a quality of "synthetic a posteriori propositions" for earthly human as "synthetic a posteriori" quality of perceptions, impressions, and opinions____realized within human Psychological Life as ego psyche metaphysical human Practical Intellect. Quality of earthly human perceptions, impressions, and opinions come to exist for early human as synthetic earthly reality idiosyncratically heresy perceptions, impression, and opinions____requiring validation via cognitive structures and cognitive process of human Mind Life intellectual evidence held as believable knowledge in human Mind Life____ "as a basketful" of ecumenical understood knowledge acquired as a lifetime spent acquiring meaningful and valuable knowledge for every earthly human____not certain set groups. Earthly human perceptions, impressions, opinions hold only earthly reality quality of one earthly human's practical and pragmatic self-centered, selfish bias based upon that quantity and that quality of acquired earthly reality information. Knowledge enables a quality processes of human Mind Life cognitive mental operations, idiosyncratic and personal to earthly human human Mind Life conscious awareness, cognitive awareness, comprehension, and understanding of human Mind Life. Knowledge, existing as personal and idiosyncratic, cannot be transferred. Knowledge is personally, uniquely, individually mentally operationally acquired as well as mentally operationally realized... and remains Human Mind Life personal knowledge. Personal and idiosyncratic knowledge exists as unique conscious awareness of an individual earthly human system of reality, system of truth, and system of belief. Personal knowledge cannot be defined as a universal truth or as a universal reality. Earthly reality information becomes universally public and remains based and biased within the perceptual awareness of its individual and idiosyncratic earthly reality information source. Earthly reality information is based and biased in perception, impression, opinion. Human Mind Life knowledge is personal, idiosyncratic, and dynamic based and biased within human Practical Intellect's interaction with psychological ego psyche interaction with phenomenally perceptual, personally impressible idiosyncratic conscious experience of earthly reality. Earthly human interacts with phenomenal earthly reality within earthly reality quality of practical and pragmatic egocentric conscious experience within an egocentric psychological need for self-satisfaction and self-gratification__void of human Mind Life intellectual evidence. Earthly reality information qualifies as the heresy as gossip; knowledge exists as intellectual evidence.

Information system. If the contemporary physical and social sciences rely upon an earthly reality Information System that supposes that the earthy reality information one scientific academic genre gathers becomes more valuable simply because that academic genre has been able to amass a greater quantity of earthly reality information than another academic genre has, as might be in the case of anthropology or sociology, where data collection can be quantified mathematically, really that qualifies that earthy reality Information System as earthly reality hearsay. Earthly reality Information Systems rely biased upon earthly realty perceptions, impressions, opinions, and unvalidated biased poll taking.

Inherent comes to exist as the essential of the actuality for **Something** to exist.

Innate exists as those intrinsic, inherent, essential essences of existence. Hereditary genes exist as physiologically innate. Mental operations exist as metaphysically innate.

Insight exists as human Mind Life innate cognitive faculty within human Mind Life mentally operational cognitive function of discernment that enables earthly human to cognitively discern in cognitive order to validate, using existing knowledge, enhancement and enrichment of intellectual evidence. Insight, becomes enhanced and enriched when autonomously and spontaneously providing meaningful value to earthly human body substance sense perception, sense impression, sense opinion capable of using innate "a priori" absolute knowledge in cognitive order to provide intellectual pre-existing intellectual evidence toward cognitive understanding earthly reality synthetic sense perceptions, sense impressions, and sense opinions as possibility of rationally functionable.

Insight initially came to exist, for the Greeks as metaphysical concept of *Anamnesis*, or, intellectual spontaneous and autonomous intuitive validation, of an earthly reality "awaiting intellectual validation" (as an "up-in-the-air" abeyance) situation, or, of an earthly reality empirically valued context provoking earthly human to validate personal and idiosyncratic system of reality, system of truth, and system of belief using human Mind Life intellectual evidence.

The Greeks, especially Plato, discussed human Mind Life metaphysical concept of Anamnesis as a human Mind Life innate "a priori" absolute metaphysical awareness of truth (Human Nature innate nous as noesis). Human Mind Life existing as nous awareness of noesis, (1) innately "a priori" knows truth, (Noumena), (2) creating new knowledge from human Mind Life cognitive function of intellectually, cognitively understanding meaning and value from earthly reality sense experiences.

Inspiration exists as a metaphysical cognitive quality of a compelling force (Henri Bergson's élan vital) within mental operations demanding linguistic and behavioral aspirational expression. Inspiration existing as a compelling force pro formance within mental operations brings forth aspiration toward linguistic and behavioral expression. Both inspiration and aspiration, existing as quality of metaphysical awareness demand human Mind Life vitality of fulfillment as intellects interact with ego psyche within earthly reality.

Instincts are natural organism dispositions innately existing within specific species of an organism expressed as biological functions automatically reacting to environmental stimuli. Instincts, existing as innate biological functions, are not learned___instincts exist innate. The prowess of instincts are necessarily conditioned by need toward survival within an environment. As example: an elephant never mates with a tiger, a tiger never mates with a lion, a gorilla never mates with a giraffe.

Integration becomes socially possible within idiosyncratic multiplies of variants within earthly human existing within earthly reality via human Mind Life mental operations of inspiration toward aspiration toward the accommodation and the assimilation of recognition and unconditionally accepted idiosyncratic multiples of variants in population thinking, in population behavior, in population language meaning, in population quantity and quality of knowledge, cognitive comprehension, and cognitive understanding of multitudes of variant earthly realities.

Intellect exists as mental operations "a priori," existing, of and by themselves, regardless of the knower and regardless of result from any sense experience or any sense perception. Mental operations, existing as quality of intellects, exist of and by themselves, however, mental operations are personally and idiosyncratically metaphysical "realized" by means of cognitive development, concept development, thought development, language development, learning, acquiring knowledge, and the sense experience and the sense perception of earthly reality. Intellect existing "a priori" in human Mind Life develops as the result of cognitive development, conscious awareness, percept to concept development, thought development, and language development. There comes to exist within intellectual development two qualities of intellect: Practical Intellect and Abstract Intellect. Ability of the mental operation of logical thought exists innately in Abstract Intellect "a priori." Reason, as mental operational ability, exists within human Mind Life "a priori." Concept of morality exists within human Mind Life "a priori." Concept of goodness exists in human Mind Life "a priori."

Intellectual intuition. Human Mind Life quality of cognitively acquired ***forethought*** becomes quality of intellectual intuition____a cognitive immediate process of human Mind Life to recognize and to realize cognitive understanding of earthly reality sense experiences as "meaningful measure."

Intellectualism exists as a notion that earthly human free wills to resolve and to direct pursuit of personal and idiosyncratic knowledge toward a level of the understanding of personal system of reality, personal system of truth, and personal system of belief toward the level of intellectual development of the possibility to cognitively reason.

Intellectual awareness exists within mental operations as self mental ability to realize innate "a priori" knowledge along with "a posteriori" acquired knowledge validly coalesced into cognitive structures and cognitive functions toward meaningful and valuable use within intellects interaction with ego psyche and with earthly reality. Intellectual awareness becomes the facilitator toward maintaining cognitive equilibrium and psychological equilibrium between intellects and psychological ego psyche interacting in phenomenal earthly reality.

Intellectual confidence, existing within mental operations, comes to exist when Abstract Intellect using intellectual evidence can overwhelm Practical Intellect's use of perceptual evidence in cognitive order to make an intelligent judgment toward an intended earthly world-wide worthy consequence.

Intellectual evidence exists as individual, idiosyncratically valued knowledge which has been stored in memory which has been personally discerned and personally freely willed to be of use toward (1) intellectual value, (2) qualitative intellectual application, (3) qualitative intellectual expression, and, (4) possible mentally, operational validation of any newly acquired knowledge. Intellectual evidence exists psychologically differently then does perceptual evidence, because, although intellectual evidence was originally acquired by means of sense experience and sense perception, and, once existed as perceptual evidence within Practical Intellect, intellectual evidence can no longer exist in the percept, because percept has been intellectually transformed into quality of abstract metaphysical concept. In Human Mind Life. Intellectual evidence has voided itself of both egocentrism and perception. Intellectual evidence exists in the Abstract Intellect as valuable, qualitative evidence of Abstract Intellect ability to store personally, meaningful knowledge. Possibility of existence of intellectual evidence requires mental operations to transform perceptually evident percept into abstract metaphysical concept. Possibility of existence of intellectual evidence requires mental operations to possess ability toward an abstract, conscience conscious awareness amongst intellects, ego psyche, and phenomenal earthly reality. Possible existence of intellectual evidence requires mental operations to transcend any self-conscious awareness that may exist between ego psyche and earthly reality. Consideration of the possible quality of intellectual evidence depends upon (1) a level of conscience conscious awareness, (2) status of personal awareness, (3) status of intellectual awareness, and, (4) status of psychological awareness.

Intellectual responsibility exists within mental operations by which an individual intellectually, by means of cognitive awareness, conscious awareness, conscience, and knowledge recognizes and realizes interaction occurring amongst intellects, ego psyche, and earthly reality.

Intelligent Design exists as a cosmological theory that there exists "ultimate prototypical principles that can explain the existence (that is) of everything (arche). **Arche** was brought forth by the Greek philosophers, BCE, carried through into Western Civilization thought by Avicenna, (980-1037 AD), Averroes, (1126-1198 AD), Maimonides, (1135-1204 AD), Aquinas, (1225-1274), Scholasticism. (1100-1700), Enlightenment philosophers, (1650-1790), beginning with Baruch Spinoza, (1632-1677), until Benjamin Franklin, (1706-1790), and,

Thomas Jefferson, (1743-1826), continuing today with the Catholic Church. Contemporary system of belief in science rejects the cosmological theory of Intelligent Design.

"In temporia" exists as metaphysical human Mind Life recognition and realization that earthy human exists within a body substance in a cosmological physical universal existence in limited space and in limited time.

Intention, as a mental operation, is an idea of a percept or of a concept directed toward a object, event, or other. Mental functions existing within the mental operation of intention include: (1) *intent* connotes a mental function of deliberation, (2) **purpose** connotes a mental function toward resolution, (3) *aim* connotes use of varying mental functions which may personally and idiosyncratically validate the intention, (4) *goal* connotes mental functions' directed resolution of the intent toward a specific behavior, psychological resolution, or intellectual evidence, and, (5) *end* connotes the mental function of free willful resolution of the intent which might be expressed by means of behavior or language, and, comes to exist as a renewed qualitative conscience conscious awareness. Intention is a cognitive thinking process that may be qualified by either cognitive awareness or perceptual awareness.

Intentionality exists within Abstract Intellect as a metaphysical phenomena using cognitive functions within a conscience conscious awareness toward effecting and affecting a self-directed goal, and, hopefully, the outcome of that goal. Intention, existing within Abstract Intellect, functions cognitively using cognitive functions, and, knowledge, toward mental operations which "hopefully" might effect and affect the "intended" outcome. The "intended" outcome would be achieved if a renewed conscious awareness occurred. Intentionality existing within Abstract Intellect functions as a cognitive means to effect and to affect qualitative enhancement and enlightenment of present conscious awareness. The "intended" outcome is to effect and to affect a renewed qualitative status of conscious awareness.

Intentional Phronesis existed for the Ancient Greeks as a metaphysical idea within philosophical speculation as ***practical wisdom***. For the Ancient Greeks, phronesis was sensible intuition using practical intelligence____not using sense perception, seems impression, sense opinion gained from sense experience of earthly reality. Practical Intellect took "mental moments" in social practical and pragmatic order to discern prudent phronesis____what to do, how to do it, in social order to cause the least harm, to achieve a common good for the most, in social order to achieve, for, the most, impartial outcome.

Intentional Wisdom exists as a very sagacious cognitive level of cognitive awareness. Wisdom can extend wisdom as intellectual intuition into earthly reality quality of ***intentional wisdom*** in cognitive praxis as a gift given as the virtue of innate knowing of insightful immediate, spontaneous, autonomous cognitive knowing of "what to empathetically do when to do it." ***Wisdom*** exists as ultimate innate knowledge of intellectual intuition which causes the effect of the virtuous praxis of ***intentional wisdom***. ***Wisdom*** exists as cognitive recognition and realization of ultimate innate knowledge of intellectual intuition. ***Wisdom*** exists as cognitive recognition and realization of ultimate innate knowledge of Human Nature. Intentional wisdom provokes "wise" practical and practical into earthly reality speak and behavior.

Virtue. Aristotle explained ***virtue*** at its best in his book, **Nicomachean Ethics**____praxis of virtue is at its best when human Mind Life understands at the right time, about the right things, towards the right people, for the right end, and, in the right way intellectual intuition of how to empathically spontaneously and autonomously behave and what to say in an immediate earthly reality space and time. ***Intentional praxis of virtue*** demands intentioned earthly reality outcome of good, moral, and reason.

Intended consequences result as meaningful measure of two qualities of cognitive awareness: matterful consequence and metaphysical awareness.

Interpretation exists within mental operations as a possibility to discern the meaning and the value of a speculative propositions by means of perception, apperceiving, insight, analysis, logic, intellectual qualities in translation of meanings, intellectual judgment, mental awarenesses, cognitive awareness, and, conscience conscious awareness.

Judgment exists as a mental ability within mental operations evoking a need to intellectually validate with already existing "a priori" knowledge any new perception of events, objects, other beings in cognitive order to discern a possibility toward the resolution within cognitive validation. The mental operation of judgment becomes necessary contingency of human Mind Life cognitive mental structures and cognitive mental functions toward the use of metaphysical thought in any problem-solving or goal-oriented earthly reality context and situation. Quality of cognitive ability, quality of cognitive structures and cognitive functions, quality of human Mind Life intellectual evidence, as well as, quality of multiple conscience conscious awarenesses come to determine quality of human Mind Life conscience conscious awareness judgment.

Justice exists both sentient and metaphysical. Metaphysically if each earthly human can bring forth a system of reality, a system of truth, and a system of belief that every human deserves respect, kindness, and appreciation, then, there would be no need to make conventional laws governing personal and idiosyncratic behavior. **Justice becomes justice when legal court judgment is no longer needed.**

Kindness, existing within mental operations, becomes the acquisition of **ultimate appreciation, and, respect for Human Nature.** All earthly humans hold the same Human Nature. That all earthly humans hold the same Human Nature makes all earthly humans equally Intelligently Designed. That which makes earthly humans unequal is that not all earthly humans Mind Life acquire the same cognitive level of the understanding.

Language exists as an earthly reality socially shared code or conventional system attempting physical sign representation of metaphysical concepts through the use of arbitrary symbols and rule-governed combinations of those symbols.

Language as thought representing personal and idiosyncratic knowledge is facilitated by earthly human personal and idiosyncratic cognitive awareness to abstract percepts into concepts____toward multiple mental awarenesses of percepts and concepts____toward a cognitive transformation of percepts into concepts____toward a perceptual awareness of percepts existing within Practical Intellect as well as a cognitive awareness of concepts existing within Abstract Intellect____ toward a comprehension of the transformation (translation) of "a meaning" held by the percept into a possible "relational meaning" held by the concept____toward an understanding that the concept might come to be represented by a word____toward "making meaning" coming to exist as linguistic expression in a given time in a given space in a given earthly reality.

Language development exists as earthly human sequential and incremental mental operational activity of acquiring the concepts of language as a representational symbol system of sense experienced and sense perceived earthly reality. Language development becomes earthly human cognitive ability to think about language, to recognize language as an entity separate from its concrete-empirical representations. Earthly human must learn to analyze word usage, to discern word meaning, to recognize content and context word meaning, to make value judgments about the use of word meaning. Earthly human must learn linguistic competence and linguistic expression. Any possibility in proficiency in language development requires linguistic competence and linguistic performance in all four mediums of language: reading and writing, speaking and listening. Learning towards development of cognition requires thought development interacting with language development. Any possibility of the use of language as thought representing personal knowledge is facilitated by earthly human personal and idiosyncratic cognitive awareness to abstract percepts into concepts toward multiple mental awarenesses difference between percepts meaning and value when referencing earthly reality, and, concepts meaning and value when referencing earthly reality.

toward a cognitive transformation of percepts into concepts... toward a perceptual awareness of percepts existing within practical intellect as well as a cognitive awareness of concepts existing within abstract intellect... toward comprehension of the transformation (translation) of "a meaning" held by the percept into a possible "relational meaning" held by the concept... toward understanding that the concept might come to be represented by a word... toward "making meaning"... coming to exist as linguistic expression in a given time in a given space in a given reality.

Law of noncontradiction, which correlates to a law of identity, suggests that "something" (existence) must come to be the "identity" (essence) of "itself" (actuality). Therefore the "something" that exists can never be the opposite of itself... it can only become the possibility of itself. However, the "one something" exists "absolutely" different from "another something," otherwise, "no something" would hold "true" identity!

Learning becomes a dynamic, cognitive developmental process which continuously occurs within the human Mind life of earthly human. *Learning* exists as an innate cognitive developmental ability of Human Nature species possessing a human Mind Life. *Learning* exists as Human Nature unfolding Human Nature into earthly reality. Earthly reality demands that earthly human, via human Mind Life, acquire learning significantly and sufficiently in cognitive order to maintain and to sustain homeostasis between Human Nature and Nature Nature. Intelligent Design never intended Human Nature to effect and to affect chaos on the universe.

Learning requires Human Nature to recognize and to realize Human Nature and Nature Nature as truth. Human Mind Life arrived into earthly reality innately "a priori" holding absolute knowledge of truth as metaphysical concepts of goodness, virtue, morality, honor, trust, decency toward earthly reality worthy principle praxis. Worthy principle in praxis demands human Mind Life conscious awareness of a system of belief in earthly reality that earthly human can learn and behave logically reasonably. Human Nature, existing in earthly reality places into rectitude praxis absolute necessary universal everlasting expression accommodation into earthly reality experiences, and, self-responsible, intelligent contribution. Human Nature earthly reality cognitive adaptation quality will effect and affect, over time and space, a quality earthly reality, by cognitive development, (as human Mind Life recognition and realization that it is human metaphysical Mind Life, as well as, a forced pro formed Human Nature of cognitive ability to mentally, operationally resolve contradictions that arise between that which human Practical Intellect perceives of earthly reality alongside that which human Abstract Intellect innately "a priori" metaphysically conceptually knows. Earthly human arrived into earthly reality pre-designed as intelligent Human Nature possessing in human Mind Life conscious awareness the absolute, necessary, universally applied essential archetypes and prototypes of Human Nature purpose and reason to exist in earthly reality. Earthly human, now existing in earthly reality, must, using human Mind Life innate "a priori" knowledge of the rectitude of significant and sufficient sublime pro formational Human Nature Intelligence bestowed upon Human Nature in both cognitive and social order to bring forth into earthly reality rectitude in probity. Earthly reality was not Intelligently Designed force pro formed to force pro form a chaotic and absurd, unkind and hated Human Nature.

Learning enables earthly human to become Human Nature Intelligently Designed. Learning enables earthly human to acquire social information to be transformed into sublime force pro formance to bestow upon earthly reality truth absolute necessary universal principles using cognitive ability of human Mind Life intellectually evident level of logical reason.

Learning enables Human Nature to recognize and to realize Human Mind Life cognitive structures and cognitive functions in cognitive order to force pro form, "to teach," earthly reality that which Human

Nature innately "a priori" knows of the essence of Human Nature existence to be manifested into phenomenal earthly reality. Phenomenal earthly reality has "no thing" to teach Human Nature. Nature Nature has been intelligently designed never to disobey Nature Nature. The ontology and the teleology of Human Nature exists as the sublime force pro formations of the creation of universe____absolutely universally essentially everlastingly true to innate "a priori" human Mind Life knowledge of "all of it." Human Mind Life holds the ecumenical; earthly reality must learn from human Mind Life. Phenomenal, uncertain earthly reality holds "no thing" knowledgeably, intellectually cognitive. Phenomenal earthly reality holds uncertainty and absurdity. ***Earthly reality holds only perceptual evidence as outreach that Human Nature must become the "teacher" of earthly reality.*** Cognitive process of learning is bestowed upon earthly reality by human Mind Life. Human Mind Life exists as the control, the power, the wealth of earthly reality. The quality of earthly reality adaptation to human Mind Life Intelligence will be determined by the quantity and by the quality of intellectual evidence an earthly human recognizes and realizes about Human Nature. Who is the king of the earthly reality jungle____the king of the earthly reality jungle is Human Nature Mind Life.

Philosophical speculation becomes a cognitive process of human Mind Life metaphysically thinking. Philosophical speculation teaches earthly reality to recognize and to realize human Mind Life. Religious dogma becomes a result of Human Spirit contemplation and meditation of Human Animus. Religious dogma teaches earthly reality status of contemplation. Science, social sciences, government, educational institutions, critical thinking of think tanks criticism of earthly reality informational "theories" fill up earthly reality with confusion and absurdity. Earthly reality corrupts human Mind Life of Human Nature. Human Mind Life of Human Nature has been intelligently designed to eliminate earthly reality absurdity and corruption.

Process of human Mind Life cognitive development toward teaching earthly reality becomes (1) cognitive development, (2) thought development, (3) language development, (4) intellectual evidence (5) psychological development, and (6) effective and affective interaction between earthly human Mind Life alongside earthly reality. Learning requires interaction amongst intellects, ego psyche, and earthly reality. Learning develops multiple mental awarenesses. Learning develops acumen in cognition, in intellectual evidence, and, in knowledge "a posteriori" acquired. Effective learning (teaching) requires attention to learning (teaching), and, human Mind Life focus attention to cognitive awareness of learning (teaching). Effective learning (teaching) requires mental cognitive focus. Earthly human needs to recognize "what he knows," as well as, "what he does not know." Qualitative intellectual discernment towards sufficiently acquiring new knowledge demands that earthly human recognizes and realizes that which "he does not know" about earthly reality's contradictions and absurdities. Earthly human needs to recognize and to fully realize when some new knowledge has been acquired from earthly reality contradictions and absurdities. If earthly human recognizes "what he knows," and, does "acknowledge" when he learns "something absolute," earthly human has "certainly" contributed to earthly reality "a learned something"____renewed conscious awareness occurs when human Mind Life can effect, and, can affect goodness, righteousness, integrity, decency, trust, truth, and reason upon earthly reality.

Learning requires a continuously developmentally abstracting process toward acquiring a multitude of logical. Reasonable "a posteriori" knowledge. Learning requires (teaching) thought development and language development. The result of learning will continue to become a personal and idiosyncratic accumulation of all-encompassing knowledge as a cognitive awareness of cognitive ability to "complete the puzzle" via cognitive faculties of comprehension, understanding, and reason. Acquiring knowledge requires human Mind Life cognitive structures and cognitive functions as human Mind Life mental operations in the transaction of transforming sense experience as idiosyncratic sense perception into human Mind Life cognitive systems of logical reason. In cognitive order to effectively learn earthly human must (1) be prepared to continually "consciously aware renew" his present cognitive status knowledge; "change" is not an event, "change" is a process, (2) to cognitively become prepared to "accept" new knowledge, (3) care and desire to "change" and "accept" new knowledge. Learning (teaching) becomes realized within cognitive structure and cognitive functions existing in human Mind Life. Learning is a developmentally abstracting process of the possibility of earthly human logically reasonably acquiring a reality system, a truth system, and a belief system____based upon absolute necessary universal principles as archetypes and prototypes of Human Nature. Earthly human continuous learning, at any point in his lifetime, may be considered his body of knowledge. Beware! Earthly reality teaches only contradiction, conflict, confusion, disrespect, criticism, and absurdity____this is that quality of earthly information which human ego psyche learns.

Linear time exists as history, as historical earthly reality time in space, and, exists as future time. Linear time exists as a conventional invention in social order to measure mental operational moments of the development of human Mind Life metaphysical concepts of past, present, and future. Linear time exists within human Mind Life metaphysical mental operations in cognitive force pro formance of cognitive memory in cognitive order to measure and to value earthly human earthly reality activity.

Linguistic cognition exists as mental operations using language as method toward symbolic, empirical representation of that which human Mind Life already knows innately "a priori." Intellectual evidence existing in human Mind Life gives meaning to language use. Communicative language can represent only that quality of knowledge already individually and idiosyncratically acquired as believable becoming knowledge, that quality cognitive development, that quality conscious awareness, that quality language development which human MindLife has already acquired. Communicated language can only representatively express earthly human "thought-filled cognitively understood significance and value."

Linguistic context always remains biased as long as language expression is not based in innate "a priori" absolute concepts human Mind Life metaphysically knows as universal categories of essential existence.

Linguistic reconstruction comes to exist as metaphysical thought linguistically constructed. Metaphysical thought moves from human Mind Life "transcendentally essential" transformed into earthly reality meaning and value "transcendentally empirical" (Jacques Derrida)____metaphysical thought empirically reconstructed into a form of language. Metaphysical thought uses metaphysical language uses conventionally culture symbolic language to emotively imagine new conscious awareness of earthly realty via (1) metaphysical thought, (2) intelligent thought, and (3) human Mind Life knowledge. Metaphysical thought expresses metaphysical thought linguistically reconstructed into conventional earthly reality symbol system symbol and signified representation as language. Earthly reality expression of metaphysical thought becomes only as good as meaningful and valuable choice words used in language expression.

Listen versus hear. "Listening" using language and thought requires (1) cognitive awareness of language and thought, (2) conscious awareness of perceptual evidence within the immediate contextual situation, and, intellectual evidence of the "message" that the other is attempting to convey, (3) cognitive discernment of the difference between perceptual evidence and intellectual evidence. Jacques Derrida, (1930-2004), suggested that language force pro forms both transcendentally empirically and transcendentally essential at the same time in in the same space in the same earthly reality, and (4) care enough to will "to listen" to metaphysical essential message using language awareness with thought awareness instead of "hearing" only his own personal perceptual evidence. Listen, existing within mental operations, is one of the four mental operations involved toward quality language development: reading, writing, talking, and listening. Language development becomes a qualitative cognitive function toward the acquisition of knowledge, especially reading and listening. Listen requires conscious awareness of cognitive awareness and psychological awareness. Sense experience of hearing merely stimulates the cognitive function of cognitive quality of listening.

Locutionary speech acts, within linguistic expression, is the actual performance utterance conditioned by its ostensible, either pretended or evident, meaning. A locutionary act uses rhetoric and phatic acts in social order to convey an earthly reality socio-political intentional persuasion toward goal of socially accepted behaviors toward the establishment of "desired" population thinking.

Logic, as a discipline, is the philosophical investigation into the possibility of reasoning by means of the use of formal language, which formal language has a set logical model of presentation, called a syllogism; logic may use mathematical symbol system as its logical model. Either model are used toward possibility of valid inference of truth within use of the syllogistic, or, mathematical language. Logical language is considered as "formal" language because of the "syllogistic form" in which the language is presented opposed to natural, normative, grammatical statement language.

"Logical parsing" exists as mental operations when intellects (practical and abstract) attempt "to make sense," "to make meaning," from reading or hearing language as that language might possibly represent a knowable, reasonable, actual reality. A sentence may represent, by means of language, intellectual schema representing a possible reality. Logical thought provokes "logical parsing" of the sentence to occur as a function of logical thought attempting meaning out of the sentence by "seeking out" any concepts of common, critical attributes, within intellect's schema in cognitive order to cognitively validate the sentence's perceptions with already stored schema toward possible "meaning" of that which the sentence might "intend" as a statement of mere earthly reality information. The critical, attributes and qualities existing in language in synthetic form of a proposition, at first, are identified by the "subject" and "verb" in the sentence. Logical thought, analytical logical thinking, logical parsing provokes thought "to seek out" the "subject" and the "predicate" (verb) of the synthetic proposition. "Who is doing it" and "what are they doing?" These two answers are critical, qualities and attributes toward "making meaning" from the sentence. After thought has discerned the "doer of the action," and that which, the "doer is doing" the other words in the sentence begin to place attributes or qualifiers placing significance and value toward making meaning of the context. The major premise in the sentence, which is the predicate, qualifies the minor premise in the sentence, which is the subject (or vice versa), both qualified by qualities and attributes that give possible validity to the synthetic proposition. Language is only as logical toward making meaning as thought is logical toward making meaning___and logic in thought supersedes any possibility of logic in language. Language never speaks or is heard! Thought speaks and is heard! What is a noun?" If you answered that "a noun is a person, place, or thing," that is incorrect. You are a person. Are you a "noun?" Your "name" is a noun! A noun is a word! What is a "noun?" A "noun" is the "name" (a word) of a person, place, or thing! Earthly reality synthetic propositions, in possibility to become believable, must be transcendently transformed from "in the moment" contextual situation into absolute everlasting meaningfulness in order to transcendentally come to exist as everlastingly essential.

Logical proposition "a posteriori" is a statement of thought that might be expressed by means of "formal" or "natural" language, or, mathematical symbol system, proposing consideration about sense experience and sense perception toward seeking affirmation by means of cognitive validation. A logical proposition "posteriori" using "formal" or "natural" language may stimulate cognitive and psychological contemplation by (1) motivation, (2) intention, (3) sense impression, (4) earthly reality sense inference, or, possibly (5) innate "a priori" logical, reasonable intellectual evidence, (6) psychological resolution toward psychological satisfaction, and, (7) need for cognitive resolution toward cognitive satisfaction.

Logical thought exists innately "a priori" as a process of human Mind Life mental operations using cognitive functions as methods toward logical, yet synthetic "a priori" deduction of the validity of the earthly reality synthetic proposition according to how the "words" are stated awaiting human Mind Life cognitive validation in cognitive order to become intellectually believable. Practical Intellect presents to Abstract Intellect an inferential (stimulated, seductive, emotive, intuitive) induction to Abstract Intellect. Human Mind Life cognitive structures and cognitive functions, as well as, human Mind Life acquired intellectual evidence (schemata) begins cognitive processes in attempt to validate sense experience and sense perception with existing schemata within human Mind Life existing as intellectual evidence (schemata). Schemas are mentally structured clusters of abstract metaphysical concepts which have been mentally operationally organized by means of categorizing commonalities and principles which could mentally represent events, objects, and other beings which have been sense experienced, and, have been abstractly stored into intellect as memory. How can I recognize a "cat" if I have not already cognitively discerned what is a "cat?" Logical reasonable thought requires the cognitive function of logical reasonable thinking. Logical reasonable thought existing as a process of human Mind Life metaphysical thinking requires the cognitive functions of deliberation, discernment, and logical reasonable judgment____necessary absolute criteria exists as the innate "a priori" sublime pro formational universal principles of contingency necessity for "something certain" to actually exist as "something certain"_____water is always water, matter is always matter, energy is always energy. Metaphysical abstract concept of "fair" innately "a priori" known in human Mind Life exists as a conceptual absolute of necessary contingency of metaphysical abstract concept of "fair" universally everlastingly "fair"_____never situationally contextualized, nor, arbitrated by any earthly reality existence temporary content. Fair is always fair__otherwise, fair is not fair____it is earthly reality anything other. Fair is not absolute metaphysical concept of "fair" when earthly reality "socio-political fair" is arbitrarily determined by an earthly reality socio-political set group. Earthly reality language "logical thought" attempts to qualify and to quantify relational interactions occurring between earthly reality information and innate "a priori" human Mind Life intellectual evidence existing as contingency necessary essential to universal absolute criteria toward metaphysical possibility that "an absolute" everlastingly remains its "absolute" essential. Good is good, otherwise, good would not be good. Moral is moral, otherwise moral would not be moral. An absolute essential of necessary contingency can only be defined by itself. You are you, and, you cannot be Peter, Paul, or Mary!

Logocentric thought exists as a cognitive quality within Human Mind Life cognitive mental operations as metaphysical conceptual thought existing independent of earthly reality sense perception of sense experience. Logocentric thought exists as human Mind Life quality to metaphysically cognitively abstract via metaphysical cognitive abstraction universal contingency necessity, in cognitive order, to recognize and to realize universal necessary absolutes everlastingly essential toward earthly human, Human Nature, and Nature Nature existence. Waters exists as always water, matter exists as always matter, energy exists as always energy. Absolutes everlastingly essentially exist in existence order toward existence.

However, unfortunately, within earthly reality, morality, as a metaphysical absolute necessary concept toward Human Nature existence in earthly reality, is NOT always earthly reality behaved as morality____reason, as a metaphysical absolute necessary concept toward Human Nature existence in earthly reality is NOT always behaved as reason. Both human ego psyche and earthly reality corrupt the absolute pureness of Human Nature. The Logos exists as the essential pureness of Human Nature human Mind Life conscious awareness of Human Nature human Mind Life ***pure*** conscious awareness. Earthly language does not exist significantly and sufficiently, in cognitive metaphysical order, to explain human Mind Life within Human Nature.

Logocentric thought resides within the Logos which cannot be known by means of earthly reality sense perception of sense experience. Logocentric thought innately holds human Mind Life cognitive mental operational ability to provoke the cognitive level of the understanding which in human Mind Life becomes knowledge-for-the sake-of-knowledge independent from any external earthly reality extensions.

Logos are metaphysical "a priori" known necessary essence of earthly reality existence.

Logocentric thought resides beyond physical earthly reality of egocentric thought and physical earthly reality of sociocentric thought. In earthly reality, unfortunately, human language exists inadequate to explain the metaphysical of human Mind Life Logocentric thought. Human Mind Life cognitive understanding of the Logos exists essentially pure of anything earthly reality could ever tell. Earthly reality language remains the only earthly reality method toward expressing human Mind Life meaning of knowledge-for-the-sake-of-knowledge. The structure of language, as sign, as symbol, in grammar, in syntax, in vocabulary, toward possibility of making meaning does enable earthly reality thought to think logically. The function of language, in semiotics, toward possibility of making meaning, however, within earthly reality, assumes a specific cultural phenomena bases and bias, as well as, personal and idiosyncratic intention expression. Use of earthly reality language assumes personal and idiosyncratic meaning representation not communicated as cognitive level of understanding. Communication of understanding between earthly humans within Logocentric language usage requires language to express Logocentric thought. Logocentric thought transcendentally transforms the "Anything earthly uncertain "into the "Something absolutely certain." Logocentric thought resides beyond earthly reality of egocentric thought and beyond earthly reality of sociocentric thought. Logocentric thought resides in, directs, and sustains human Mind Life as Human Nature.

Logos, for the ancient Greeks, connoted a terminology for that conceptual ability of human Mind Life, as Abstract Intellect, to acquire human Mind Life cognitive mental operational function toward cognitive level of the understanding____ that which sense experience and sense perception of earthly reality cannot ever physically come to experience. (Immanuel Kant).

Mathematics. Mathematics exists as a human Mind Life "Known Known." The expression of metaphysical absolute concepts of

Mathematics, does not require "a posteriori" knowledge learned by earthy human in cognitive order to acquire learning of Mathematics. Mathematics speaks, into earthly reality, metaphysical language expression of human Mind Life logical reason. Recognizing and realizing principles of Mathematics exists as human Mind Life earthly expression of human Mind Life logical reason. Conventional socio-cultural-political earthly reality synthetic language existing as socio-cultural-political arbitrary meaning as biased based agreement of a socio-cultural-language, which cannot represent human Mind Life logical reasoning. Mathematical linguistic symbolization language does. Mathematical discernments can represent truth; conventional socio-cultural-political language serves no truth *Matter* exists as earthly reality existing within Nature Nature.

Matter-filled consequence ethics is that notion of applied earthly reality ethics that might be concerned with "getting caught." A behavior as a decision remains "good" and not "wrong" as long as "I do not get caught!"

Matter-filled consequence, coming to exist as a result of intellectual status within Abstract Intellect causes Abstract Intellect to constitute a status of cognitive disequilibrium and cognitive dissatisfaction which status now reflects itself in non-qualitative, cognitive interaction manifested in earthly reality behavior or language amongst Practical Intellect alongside ego psyche within earthly reality. Matter-filled consequence may result as personal self-consciousness. Abstract Intellect, existing as intellectual evidence, cannot resolve earthly reality contradictions and absurdities between that which ego psyche is perceiving when interacting with earthly reality. Ego psyche's Practical Intellect resolves that ego psyche and earthly reality are winning! Because ego psyche, as Practical Intellect, will not meet Abstract Intellect existing as human Mind Life____ego psyche and earthly reality are winning!

Matter-filled consequence, coming to exist as a result of psychological, practical, and pragmatic status within Practical Intellect, causes Practical

Intellect to constitute a status of cognitive disequilibrium and cognitive dissatisfaction which status now reflects itself in non-qualitative, cognitive interaction represented by social behavior, or, by social Acts of Speech. Acts of Speech reveal the self-centeredness of ego psyche. Matter-filled consequence may result as personal self-consciousness of ego psyche because of lack of sufficient knowledge to resolve either psychological or cognitive intent. Practical Intellect, existing as psychological ego psyche, cannot resolve the contradictions between that which ego psyche is perceiving interacting with earthly reality. Practical Intellect perceives that ego psyche and earthly reality are winning!

Matter-filled consequence, coming to exist as a result of psychological status within ego psyche, causes ego psyche to constitute a status of psychological disequilibrium and status of psychological dissatisfaction which status now reflects itself within ineffective and un affective consequential, practical (as praxis with earthly reality) behavior and language. Matter-filled consequence may result as personal self-consciousness. Ego psyche perceives himself as the dominant actor interacting within Practical Intellect interacting with earthly reality, but, nevertheless, "refuses" to get involved with Abstract Intellect! Earthly reality corrupted is wining!

Matter-filled consequence may come to exist as "momentary meaningful experience"... in the moment in earthly reality earthly reality perception may come to be precariously validated by a previous perception... and... come to give momentary psychological satisfaction... however... human Mind Life cognitive level at this moment in earthly reality remains egocentric because ego psyche relies upon earthly reality perception toward ego psyche's validation... "all that matters" is that which momentarily matters!" Ego psyche has not developed beyond interacting with earthly reality egocentrically. Ego psyche remains non-qualitatively cognitively involved as ego psyche dominates interaction with earthly reality with no regard for Abstract Intellect's intellectual evidence. "Ego" perceptually deceives himself that he is being validated by the possession of an object, or by the attendance at an event, or by another. Cognitive equilibrium and cognitive satisfaction and psychological equilibrium and psychological satisfaction demand that "ego psyche perceiving" validate ego psyche "perceiving" with Abstract Intellect using intellectual evidence in cognitive order to validate perception, impression, opinion. Earthly reality information can never come to validate earthly human perceptions, impressions, opinions. Responsible consequence comes to exist within human Mind Life mental status as cognitive equilibrium, cognitive satisfaction, psychological equilibrium, and psychological satisfaction when Abstract Intellect, using intellectual evidence, can come to validate earthly reality perceptions, impressions, and opinions. Matterful consequence may result as "an unintended consequences" because ego psyche chose not interact with Abstract Intellect. Ego psyche and earthly reality are winning!

Meaning becomes a differentiated conscious awareness that arbitrarily develops within earthly human as a result of discretionary cognitive mental operations and psychological mental awarenesses based upon cognitive awareness and becomes substantively related to earthly human cognitive structure and cognitive functions. Seeking meaning becomes earthly human personal idiosyncratic cognitive mental motivation "to make sense" of earthly human relationship between earthly human and earthly reality. Earthly human personal idiosyncratic mental operation of acquiring personal idiosyncratic *meaning* is related to the quality of earthly human Mind Life ability to logically reason earthly reality "non sense" with Practical Intellect practical and pragmatic perception sense____ voiding seeking *meaning* held innately "a priori" in human Mind Life. ***Meaning arrives within human Mind Life renewed conscious awareness of cognitive function of the understanding. Cognitive function of the understanding holds knowledge awareness for knowledge awareness____voided of earthly reality perceptions, impressions, opinions. Cognitive function of the understanding does not understand earthly human synthetic perceptions, impressions, and opinions. Earthly human synthetic perceptions, impressions, opinions are bound tightly to earthly reality uncertain happenstance____earthly human fateful Demiurge. Demiurge exists as earthly reality fatefully uncertain happenstance. There is meaning*** *to be discovered in the earthly reality fateful uncertain Demiurge. Earthly human must meet earthly human Mind Life.*

"Meaningful measure" comes to be realized either in practical intellect or in abstract intellect when "some" measure of *quantity* of experiences, or, of quantity of perceptions, or, of quantity of knowledge transforms into "some" measure of *quality* of experiences, or, quality of perceptions, or, quality of knowledge. "Meaningful measure" comes to be realized when "nothing" "significantly," but, "suddenly" becomes human Mind Life quality of cognition as "something understood."

Measure is a conceptual notion presented by Georg Wilhelm Friedrich Hegel, (1770-1831), proposed as "measure" of quantity of earthly reality perception with quality of Abstract Intellect intellectual evidence. Hegel's "measure" ran along a nodal line (points on a axis) whereby a quantum of intellectual evidence arrived "suddenly," but, "significantly!" There may come to exist so much quantity of earthly reality perceptual evidence within Practical Intellect as "to seem" to put at abeyance the possibility of quality of human Mind Life intellectual evidence in cognitive order "to change quantity perceptions into quality intellectual evidence!" Because Practical Intellect "interacts nodally" on a "transcendentally linear line" interacting with Abstract Intellect, quantity can change into quality "suddenly," but, "significantly" within epicycles of the correlational contact of Practical Intellect interacting with Abstract Intellect within earthly time suspended _____ transcendental transaction between human Practical Intellect and human Abstract Intellect occurs within human Mind Life "mental moments." Human Mind Life knows not earthly time, nor, does human Mind Life require "a measure of earthly time." A qualitative quantum of knowledge "surfaces" as Spinoza's process of human Mind Life intellectual intuition that suddenly, spontaneously, autonomously permits human Mind Life reason to grasp that knowledge needed as intellectual evidence in cognitive order "to metaphysically realize" "concepts!" Hegel held notion, that, within a process of understanding, thought will cease becoming and just become. Both Spinoza and Hegel believed that human intellects (as metaphysical concepts) superseded ego psyche earthly reality time bound practical and pragmatic percepts (as synthetic propositions) of earthly reality. Cognitive mental operation of "realize" results as "measure" of "trans space." Metaphysical absolute concepts of certainty (matter, energy, force, good, kind) speak truth; earthly reality synthetic perceptions, impressions, opinions speak lies. A quantum physics scientist might give contemplation to the wave-like behavior of the atom in the atom's need to maintain and to sustain the atom. Water must always be water____or it is anything else. Nature Nature may never disobey itself. Human Nature must always be Human Nature____however Human Nature is compromised in earthly reality when psychological Practical Intellect ego psyche and free will non-intellectually interacts with earthly reality.

Memory exists as a quality and a capacity within human Mind Life mental operations enabling earthly human Mind Life to store personally cognitively acquired knowledge which has been cognitively discerned to be meaningful and valuable. Knowledge worth keeping! Quality of cognitive mental operations of emotion and imagination may discern meaning and value, orderliness, and sagaciousness of the knowledge to be stored. Cognitive mental operation of memory may process the characteristic of meaningful selection of valued learning toward acquisition of new learning as well as the use of memory integrated with emotion and imagination towards meaningful association toward acquiring new learning. Another characteristic of human Mind Life cognitive memory is that quality of long-term memory may have been emotionally and imaginatively mediated. Cognitive memory of human Mind Life possesses emotional and imaginative characteristics which mediate memory's meaning and value.

Memory Selective. Human Mind Life emotionally and imaginatively *selected* memory, revalued by emotion, and, enhanced by imagination, though not necessarily becoming pathological, rather, becomes *selective memory* emotionally valued and imaginatively enhanced toward the rethinking and retelling of past earthly reality experiences. Earthly human Practical Intellect, holding tight to ego psyche and to free will, mediates knowledge stored into memory which may come to place emphasis upon unpleasantly, emotionally valued recall, may result in neurotic thought, even possibly psychotic thought. Earthly human knowledge stored into cognitive memory which may come to be imaginatively enhanced may result in ingenuous and sagacious renewed conscious awareness. Memory, integrated with emotion and imagination, are mental operational processes occurring within the cognitive development of the mental operations of abstraction, cognitive awareness, associative learning, comprehension, understanding, and reasoning effecting and affecting a quality of cognitive development and psychological development. Memory may also cognitively manifest a capacity of human Mind Life toward qualitative realization of "a priori" innate metaphysical archetypes and prototypes which may come to be metaphysically, cognitively realized as recognition of their existence in earthly reality (Carl Jung). Quality of human Mind Life memory may hold equality of Practical Intellect, as well as, may hold quality of Abstract Intellect.

Mental faculties may be scientifically regarded as the physiological mental property of earthly human body substance, called organ brain, existing within human body substance, or, may be reasonably regraded as the metaphysical essence of the human existing as metaphysical cognitive mental operations in human Mind Life. Mental faculties include collective unconscious awareness, conscious awareness, cognitive awarenesses, intellectual awareness, psychological awarenesses, and conscience____as well as, multitudes of other cognitive mental faculties.

"Mental moments" exist within human Mind Life cognitive mental operations as "time trans spaced"____earthly reality time has cognitively mentally been placed in suspension. Memory behaves as "the clock" of cognitive mental operations. "Mental moments" begin to "trans space" Hegel's "nodal line" permitting "a posteriori" primary percepts to intersect with "a priori" secondary concepts. "A posteriori" primary percepts and "a priori" secondary concepts rise and fall within epicycles along the nodal line attempting "some measure" of human Mind Life intellectual validation. At "mental moments" validation is "placed in abeyance" awaiting the "sudden," but, "sufficient" transactional contact which might permit cognitive validation toward some meaningful measure of newly acquired knowledge. Thinking and learning are very much cognitive mental operations occurring during these "mental moments."

Mental operations may be categorized as (1) thought and language developmental, (2) cognitive developmental, (3) psychologically developmental, and (4) metaphysically attainable. Mental operations occur within human Mind Life as cognitive structure and cognitive functions.

Metaphysics is that branch of philosophy concerned with reasonably explaining Human Nature of earthly human existing and interacting in earthly reality. The metaphysician attempts to understand the "beyond scientific validation" principles and prototypes by which human Mind Life comes to know events, objects, and other beings existence in a relationship in time in space in an earthly reality, interactional cause and effect between earthly human and earthly reality, as well as, earthly human Mind Life cognitive faculty possibilities. Metaphysics is the branch of philosophy that seeks "first principles" which may explain Human Nature as an earthly reality human "being in an earthly reality." The central branch of metaphysics is ontology which is an investigation into Earthly Reality Nature (existence), actuality of Human Nature, and, ultimate possibility (essence)____as "what essentially is earthly reality existence as a Human Nature essences in an earthly reality."

Metaphysical awareness comes to develop within human Mind Life cognitive mental operations as a transcendental quality of thought between human Practical Intellect and human Abstract Intellect_____ seeking understanding. Metaphysical awareness comes to exists when human Mind Life realizes that thought can realize "beyond physical relative realities." Metaphysical awareness exists when Practical Intellect alongside Abstract Intellect acquires realization of conscious awareness toward seeking seeking understanding. Metaphysical awareness becomes the ultimate cognitive awareness within conscious awareness coming to exist as the metaphysical, cognitive realization of the metaphysically, cognitively realized principles as archetypes and prototypes as true, meaningful, and valuable toward cognitively understanding the essential functioning of critical commonalities existing as the orderliness in Human Nature and in Nature Nature_____ as compared to the disorderliness of the human condition in earthly reality.

Metaphysical essentials exist "a priori" innately known within human metaphysical Mind Life as conceptual archetypes and prototypes toward potentiality of possibility of actuality of Human Nature essential existence within an earthly reality.

Metaphysical genesis comes to exist as Human Nature cognitively conceptual metaphysical ability to recognize and to realize Human Nature spiritual essential Human Nature_____as force pro formed purpose and reason.

Metaphysical idealism speculates that any ontological reason, or, teleological purpose of the existence of Human Nature existing in an earthly reality as actuality or possibility of existence must be sustained as a metaphysical awareness in human Mind Life.

Metaphysical Language. What is metaphysical language? The actuality exists that all language that expresses metaphysical Human Mind Life metaphysical thought exists within the abstract metaphysical; and, all thought exists in the abstract metaphysical. Human Mind Life holds a unique quality of language_____metaphysical concepts. Human Mind Life "thinks" itself using metaphysical language called abstract concepts. Human Mind Life thinks human Mind Life in abstract concepts. In cognitive actuality, human Mind Life accepts earthly reality physical language as sign and symbol earthly reality representation of human Mind Life abstract concepts. Earthly humans accept physical language in social order to communicate human Mind Life metaphysical abstract thinking. Human Mind Life metaphysically thought initiates and bestows meaningful measure up on earthy reality language____else physical language would exist as mere squiggles on the page, or, as sound heard in the air. And! In social order for two people to transfer communicative thoughtful meaning, both earthly humans should comprehend the language spoken. Ideal linguistic communication could occur if both earthly humans held the same perceptions, impression, opinions of the subject under discussion. However, ideal communication of metaphysical thought held by one earthly human communicated to another earthly human is impossible____a semblance gist of the metaphysical idea possibly is comprehended____because language does not think. Human Mind Life thinks; human Mind Life thinks metaphysically in abstract concepts____human Mind Life attempting to convey abstract concept using squiggle earthly reality language. Metaphysical language speaks absolute abstract concepts____peace, reason, logic, kindness, love, care, trust, decency, respect, rectitude in probity. Earthly vulgar language speaks disrespect for metaphysical language.

Human Mind Life speaks to itself in abstract concepts. Metaphysical concepts are transcendently transferring to other metaphysical concepts within cognitive processes of association, accommodation, assimilation, cognitive satisfactory acceptance. Good is speaking to evil. Polite is speaking to rude. Kind is speaking to unkind, fair is speaking to unfair, happy is speaking to unhappy____Earthly human attempts to communicate absolute abstract concepts to each other using physical squiggles____in cognitive attempt to transform earthly human profane social awareness into rectitude in probity.

Animal species do not need to communicate with each other using physical squiggles. Animals communicate thought directly to thought.

Metaphysical language exists as abstract concept language____abstract concept speaks to abstract concept. Immanuel Kant, (1724-1804), argued that earthly humans cannot come to know "the actual" of earthly reality because the actual of earthly reality exists only in human Mind Life as the Noumena absolute truth. The abstract concept of ideal good can only be the abstract concept of ideal good____or, it would not be ideal good. However, within multitude of earthly reality (real) Phenomena of earthly human perceptions, impressions, and opinions that define "what is" earthly reality, make earthly reality a Phenomena because earthly reality never exists as the "ideal" that human Mind Life innately knows. Thus the Phenomena of Earthly Reality causes a Phenomena of Earthly Reality Language.

Edmund Husserl, (1859-1938), suggested that the nature of earthly reality physical language squiggles present a tremendous conundrum of phenomenology epoche nature of earthly reality physical language____ as a suspension of judgement. Human sense experience is placed "in abeyance" until cognitive validation is bestowed upon the metaphysical meaning of the earthly reality sense experience; a sense experience merely qualified by profane, phenomenal, non-absolute earthly reality. Earthly reality corrupts. Earthly human must meet human Mind Life.

Phenomenology epoche nature of earthly reality physical language (the need for human Mind Life to place sense experienced earthly reality language in suspension of judgment until cognitively validated by metaphysical language) came from the Ancient Greeks. The Ancients Greeks suggested that difficulty in the earthy reality use of physical language presented tremendous conundrum toward comprehensive communication of human Mind Life metaphysical thought because earthly reality language may represent "anything earthly real," however, for each earthly human the "anything earthly real" meant "something actually different" then that which human Mind Life innately "a priori" knew. The Ancient Greeks suggested that while earthly humans speak language to each other, in cognitive order, for communication to possibly occur, there needed to be "pauses in suspension of judgment as epoche," in cognitive order to contemplate the distinctive merit of the message the speech act was attempting to convey. Husserl placed great value upon earthly human intentionality toward valuing distinctive merit in speech acts. Kant placed great value upon the Noumena innately held in human Mind Life____as did Plato's Forms, Aristotle's Universals, Jung's Archetypes____validating earthly reality speech acts as actually truth acts of knowledge.

Jacques Derrida, (1930-2004), suggested that the nature of earthly reality language exists within two distinctive merit values. Earthly reality language speaks both transcendentally empirical and transcendentally essential at the same time language is used to communicate a human Mind Life Ideal concept. The listener, especially, must focus cognitive attention upon these two characteristics of language usage. Language transcendentally essential holds a distinctive merit value incorruptible because transcendental essential language speaks metaphysical absolute concepts. Language transcendently empirical speaks earthly reality perceptions, impressions, opinions corrupted by phenomenal earthly reality.

Metaphysical prototypical archetypes exist as intrinsic necessary essential of humanness.

Metaphysically realized exists as metaphysical human Mind Life recognizing and realizing innate knowns "a priori" conceptual archetypes and prototypes of a possibility of a "should be" Human Nature existence in a personally and idiosyncratically perceived earthly reality.

Metaphysical thought comes to develop within mental operations when human Mind Life uses theoretical thought brought forth as metaphysical quality thought, of and by itself, in cognitive order to recognize and to realize some meaningful measure of newly acquired conscious awareness coming to exist as intellectual evidence. Metaphysical thought provoked metaphysical thought in cognitive order to acquire new consciously aware valuable and meaningful metaphysical thought. Within metaphysical thought, metaphysical thought is only aware of itself thinking metaphysical thought.

Metaphysical unpredictable consequences become new intellectual contradictions requiring cognitive resolution toward renewed conscious awareness within metaphysical awareness that has been provoked by the dynamic relativity existing when perceiving a phenomena earthly reality.

Metaphysical validation exists within mental operations when intellect "a priori" cognitively validates cognitive resolution using metaphysically realized conceptual archetypes and prototypes of actual essential existence.

Metaphysical vocabulary exists as the absolute universal necessary innately "a priori" known absolute universal necessary knowns existing only within human Mind Life. Human Mind Life categorizes, organizes, recognizes, realizes earthly reality, Nature Nature, as well as, self by means of these absolute universal necessary innate "a priori" knowns____shape, color, size, numbers, language, ethnicity, good, evil, moral, trustful, decency, integrity, kind, rude, et el______

Mind exists as the essence of Human Nature existence possessing human Mind Life mental operations, cognitive awareness, conscious awareness, conscience, and innate "a priori" knowledge.

Mind exists as the essence of Human Nature existence possessing human Mind Life mental operations, cognitive awareness, conscious awareness, conscience, and innate "a priori" knowledge. Mind exists as cognitive mental operations conscious awareness of himself. The body substance does not have such privilege. The body substance does not possess a conscious awareness of that which the body substance does. Body substance can only have a conscious experience of that which body substance does. Body substance conscious (sense) experiences may come to acquire a sense perception of sense experience by means of practical mind "associatively sensing," "inferentially inducing," and "sensibly intuiting" that which body substance sense experiences. Contemporary system of belief in science defines sense perception as the body substance "experiencing a conscious experience"... no human Mind Life involved... either practical or abstract.

Mind exists as the essence of Human Nature existence possessing human Mind Life mental operations, cognitive awareness, conscious awareness, conscience, and innate "a priori" knowledge. Mind transcendentally transforms "nothing" into "something." That which perception (ego psyche) begins to perceive of a sense experience initially moves into status of abeyance (suspension in time and space) remaining as "synthetic a posteriori," as potentiality to become "something" (newly acquired, cognitively, intellectually validated knowledge meaningful and valuable to both intellects (practical and abstract) becoming that by virtue of Human Nature reason and purpose to exist). Human Mind Life metaphysical thought transformed "nothing" into "something." "Nothing" could have remained "anything earthly uncertain," however, human Mind Life metaphysical thought transcendentally transformed "nothing" or "anything earthly uncertain" into "something absolute" both meaningful and valuable toward both intellects (practical and abstract) becoming that by virtue of Human Nature reason and purpose to exist. Human Mind Life exists as a metaphysical awareness of human Mind Life. Human Mind Life exists as a metaphysical awareness discovering Human Nature encapsulated within a human body substance interacting within a phenomenal earthly reality. There is no dualism between human Mind Life and human body. There is no "dual!" There is a sustenance____human Mind Life sustains human body and human body sustains human Mind Life____except that human Mind Life maintains human Mind Life essence everlastingly.

Mind exists as a cognitive mentally operational awareness of human Mind Life. Human body substance does not have that privilege. Human body substance is not consciously aware of what is happening in human body substance when human body substance behaviorally reacts to stimuli, eats, sleeps, smells, tastes. Contemporary science is attempting to figure this out. Medical science takes tests, x-rays, blood panels, mammograms, MRI's, cat scans, pet scans in medical order to attempt to determine what is going on in human body substance over time in space as human body substance interacts with earthly reality.

Mind Life exist as the essence of Human Nature existence as innate, "a priori" ontological potential of becoming its teleology.

Morality, innately known "a priori" within human Mind Life cognitive mental operations, definition of what is Human's intelligently intended sublime pro formational Nature, becomes a mentally operational quality within the cognitive developmental level of human Mind Life mental operational process of reason. At that level of human Mind Life mental operations when Abstract Intellect can "realize (Logically) reason, there may not exist socially conditioned perceptual, ego psyche psychological selfish goals influencing human Mind Life abstract, absolute concept of morality. There may not exist perceptual nor psychological idiosyncrasies. Neither reason nor morality are idiosyncratic. Morality, like reason is "recognizing and realizing" the difference between right and wrong. How does an earthly human "know" the difference between right and wrong? An earthly human innately "a priori" knows moral. Earthly reality does not know moral____there exists abstract concepts in earthly reality only when human Mind Life recognizes and realizes abstract concepts in earthly reality. Such cognitive awareness requires level of cognitive awareness of reason and of moral. Reason exists as a quality level of human Mind Life cognitive development. Moral exists as an absolute, never earthly reality conditioned, innately "a priori" within human Mind Life needing to be intelligently recognized and realized as absolute abstract concept of morality. Morality exists as an absolute truth; truth can never be earthly reality perceptually, idiosyncratically defined or conditioned. Earthly human perceptually rationalized behaves moral; earthly human applies moral as earthly human pleasures human ego psyche; ignorant earthly human, who has never arrived at cognitive level of reason, does not recognize and realize absolute, abstract concept of moral.

Momentary meaningful experience comes to exist "in temporia" within practical intellect when a sense perception of a sense experience "seems" to give immediate psychological satisfaction to ego psyche interacting with earthly reality.

Motivation is a mental operation strongly directed by human Mind Life cognitive mental operation of intent and human Mind Life cognitive mental function of purpose toward effecting and affecting a cognitive and psychological resolution of intent and purpose.

Motive, existing within human Mind Life cognitive mental operations, brings forth a human Mind Life provocation to act, or, to react to earthly reality stimuli. Human Mind Life *motive* cognitively forms as a quality of a percept, or, as a quality of a concept, that has been stimulated by an immediate earthly reality content and context situation toward either a perceptual decision, a willful judgment, or, a cognitive resolution between that which ego psyche is psychologically perceiving of earthly reality and that human Mind Life is conceiving of earthly reality. Human Mind Life, functioning a *motive*, cognitively mentally operationally needs to resolve by means of language expression and/or behavioral manifestation conscious awareness of "a what should be" with "a what is" within earthly reality.

Nature versus nurture exists as the contradictions human Mind Life recognizes and realizes existing within earthly reality that require coalescing that which human Mind Life "conceives" (a priori knows) of Human Nature, and, that which earthly human consciously experiences of earthly reality.

Natural (normative) language exists as "standard" or "conventionally appropriated as the norm," however, always expressing personal and idiosyncratic meaning and values which have uniquely been established within earthly human systems of reality, systems of truth, and systems of belief, and, which language usage within a society "seems" appropriate toward intent and purpose of reciprocal communication____based and biased upon "seems." *Natural (normative) language* uses "specifically defined norms" as bases toward reciprocal communicative linguistic expression. However, this theory of language assumes that all earthly humans share the same "belief system" that the community using this natural, normative language uses. Social scientists, such as Noam Chomsky, (1928-), W.V.O. Quine, (1908-2000), Richard Rorty, (1931-2007), had suggested methods within linguistics, within neurolinguistics, and within social scientific paradigms as possibility to come to structure language that might generate relational resemblance of language to thought. Voiding normative language of all traditional metaphysical, ontological, epistemological vocabulary (vocabulary representing abstract metaphysical language) might enable sense perception of sense experience to validate "the newly determined normed language." Any considerations toward the notions of Jean Piaget's, (1896-1980), thought to language, and, of Lev Vygotsky's, (1896-1934), language to thought were completely dismissed. Contemporary social sciences morphed language structure and public sphere social vocabulary in attempt to establish language as the tool in social order to indoctrinate social thought, not as Lev Vygotsky had suggested that it was human Mind Life that determined human Mind Life metaphysical thought using language as an earthly reality tool. Contemporary social science believes that the "proper" language could come to determine social thought, thus a socially normed awareness. Contemporary "grammatically logical" system of language would come to generate socially aware earthly reality thought; logical reasonable language did not generate contemporary desired social awareness. There did not come to be accepted by these cognitive linguistic social scientists that each earthly human develops his own uniquely personal and idiosyncratic system of reality, system of truth, and system of belief. Contemporary linguistic social scientists determined that a "transformational generative grammar" could come (1) to generate desired social awareness, (2) to generate same social awareness within every earthly human (3) to communicate same social awareness "equally" shared amongst each earthly human, and, (4) avoid theoretical metaphysical thought. Georg Wilhelm Friedrich Hegel's theoretical suggestions of earthly reality contradictions between Practical Intellect and Abstract Intellect agrees with Johannes Kepler's theoretical theory of incommensurability, and, Richard Rorty's theoretical theory of "ironism!"

NATURAL SELECTION exists as a "NON-RANDOM" biological evolutionary process within humans "dependent upon and determined by" genome which represents the heredity information of an individual within his DNA and his RNA. Genomic studies the global interrelationship of genomes existing in the organism; whereas, genetics studies the properties of specific genes. The genotype represents the hereditary makeup of a cell; whereas, a phenotype represents the non-hereditary make up of a cell. Genotype (G) + environment (E)

+ genotype and environment (GE) = phenotype. Natural selection may operate "purposely functional" upon heritable traits (genotype) because hereditary seems to participate more influentially in the evolutionary process. Natural selection seems to operate "blindly" upon non-hereditary traits (phenotype). This causes genetic scientists to conclude that phenotype physical and behavioral characteristics are non-hereditary likely influenced by environment. Natural selection may be the result of an individual's unique genotype + phenotype adaptability to environment. Nevertheless, science defines natural selection as "non-random." Genotype, since determined by heredity might be notion of "non-random" evolution, color of skin may be considered as determined by heredity, however, individual and personal conditions of the birth of a human organism must be scientifically considered as idiosyncratic accidents of human birth... otherwise science is entering into a metaphysical question of pre-determination by statement that natural selection is "non-random!" Phenotype, since determined by socio-cultural environment, can posit "some" possible consideration of notion of "non-random," however, if science suggests that genotype (heredity) also "non-randomly" determines human organism, how does science explain the idiosyncrasy of human behaviors, not withstanding the idiosyncrasy of human knowledge. So science suggests that human organism becomes determined by the quality of the nature of his forefathers as well as the quality of the nature of the environment of his forefathers. Science suggests that there is no such mental function, existing as mental property within body substance, as notion of "free will." Science is suggesting that idiosyncratic human behavior and idiosyncratic human knowledge are determined by natural selection?! The human organism has no "free will" to acquire his own personal and idiosyncratic individually existing knowledge. Again science enters into metaphysical question of pre-determination. If something exists "non-randomly" then it must be concluded that it exists as a pre-determination. Notion of "free will" is not a consideration within theory of natural selection because in theory of natural selection human organism adapts to environment conditioned upon organisms physiological ability to adapt adequately to environment. It becomes an organism's physiology that comes to determine what an individual does, not the individual existing as notion of "intelligent being"... according to contemporary day scientific theory that natural selection is "non-random!" If in the case that science, as medicine, determines that human organism would be well-advised to heed certain disciplinarily health behaviors toward optimal environmental adaptation, then, "something" within human organism "needs" to make "mental consideration." "What" is it existing within human organism's genes, whether existing as genotype or phenotype, that makes that "choice?" Human organism may be determined "non-randomly" by means of theory of natural selection, and, human organism may merely exist as physiological human organism since physiological human organism becomes pre-determined by natural selection... however... there exists more to "human" than his physiology! Within a metaphysical consideration of the theory of natural selection as non-random, then it is nature that determines the human organism existing as genotype, and, it is nurture, in the form of socio-cultural indoctrination, the determines the human organism existing as phenotype. Since phenotypes may be determined nutritively by means of a socio-cultural indoctrination, and, there exists no mental function called "free will," then, individual human intelligence comes to have absolutely nothing to do with the evaluation of the nurturing being given. Contemporary science proposes that, with the aid of government, science will "need" to direct indoctrination of human phenotypes toward "optimal" human behaviors. Furthermore, what ever happened to Herbert Spencer, (1820-903), notion of "survival of the fittest"... within notion of "survival of the fittest"... consideration necessarily moves toward the ontological nature of existence and the possibility of existence as qualities of genotypes and of phenotypes... as notion of "randomness" within natural selection... how can "something" become biologically "non-randomly" determined when it is being biologically "randomly" determined "by virtue of the survival of the fittest!?" Even the events of life and death are "randomly" determined "by virtue of the nature of accident of birth or death!?"

Natural Philosophy. In the beginning, in the cradle of the Greeks' notion of philosophy, philosophy included the study of the natural sciences because the Greek word "scientia" meant "knowledge," and philosophy meant "the love of wisdom." Philosophy developed the study of natural phenomena as that natural phenomena related to human existence, human knowledge acquisition toward the development of the nature of human, the nature of human values, the significance and purpose of human, as might be mentally operationally reasonably recognized and realized into human behaviors and language expression. Both Plato, (423-347), and, Aristotle, (384-322), distinguished the study of philosophy as intrinsic knowledge of metaphysical quality toward coming to know earthly reality, as opposed to science, science as a body of knowledge which dealt with the extrinsic, physical nature of earthly reality. Whereas the study of philosophy qualitatively speculated the nature of human interacting with the phenomena of earthly reality, scientific study placed quantity of measurement, experiment, and data collecting in its consideration of human interacting with the phenomena of earthly reality. Thomas Aquinas, (1225-1274), would envelop the philosophy of Aristotle and the studies of Albertus Magnus, (1206-1280), which included alchemy, astrology, physiology, phrenology, botany, and zoology, incorporating these disciples with the study of theology establishing Medieval Scholasticism. During the Copernicus, (1473-1543), Galileo, (1564-1642), Newton (1642-1727), Age of Science, study of science began to take on more of a notion of physical phenomena referencing less the metaphysical. Renee Descartes, (1596-1650), would embrace both the metaphysical and the physical in attempt to explain their connection. Robert Boyle, (1627-1691), suggested that natural (empiricism) science could not void itself of the metaphysical nature of the physical nature of the human-reality connection. In the 20th century Ernst Mayr, (1904-2005), would return to Aristotle's notion of teleology (final cause) as well as Kant's notion of "reflective judgment" when considering the human-reality connection. Modern emphasis upon notion of Natural Philosophy beleaguers itself with scientific and sociological control of nature (environment as well as human) lessening any notion that human activity has any "worthy" metaphysical interaction with earthly reality.

Nodal line, as a "conceptual notion" of a concept of possibility toward acquiring knowledge, refers to the possibility of a "transcendentally linear progression of the two points, practical intellect connecting with abstract intellect, within axis of epicycles attempting to transverse each other." The two points, practical intellect and abstract intellect, "arrive at transcendental contact" within epicycles of thought. Epicycles exist as "swirls" of thoughts attempting contact. Georg Wilhelm Friedrich Hegel's, (1770-1831), notion of "nodal line" is a conceptual explanation of "something" that Hegel used to explain "transcendentally abstractly" a possible relationship between practical intellect (Hegel's Objective Mind) and abstract intellect (Hegel's Subjective Mind).

Nomothetic explains the terminology used within processing and establishing law(s). The Ten Commandments exist as a prime example of a nomothetic process of defining the laws of earthly human behavior.

"No thing" exists within human Mind Life as a metaphysical abstract concept that there could possibly exist "no thing" as opposed to existing "something." Philosophical and mathematically "no thing" could become "something."

Notion, existing as a percept or as a concept, may be a possibility of a system of reality, a system of truth, and a system of belief. Noumena is Immanuel Kant's terminology for that which is unknowable by means of perception. Kant's Noumena is unknowable by means of perception; can only be knowable within transcendental metaphysical abstract intellect.

Nous. For the Ancient Greeks, *Nous,* meant human Mind Life intellect. Human Mind Life cognitive ability "to come to know."

Objective exists as a mental quality to perceive events, objects, other beings in such a manner as that the immediate affected perception of events, objects, other beings can be validated with already existing metaphysical absolute concepts.

Ontic relates to "the real," and not, to "the phenomenal."

Ontology, as a discipline of metaphysics, is philosophic investigation into the nature of earthly reality (existence), actuality (being), and ultimate possibility (essence).

Ontology, given scientific definition of notion of ontology, considers that earthly reality cannot come to be known by human Mind Life by means of the use of metaphysical abstract concepts (Aristotle's universals that substantiate earthly reality), therefore, earthly reality always remains as a phenomenological awareness of quality of "sensible intuition," or, John Stuart Mills's, (1806-1873), "inferential induction" or "perceptual judgment," as Mill's suggestion that knowledge of earthly reality always remains uncertainly relative. Husserl suggested the difference in the two phenomenological methods, "sensible intuition" (scientific ontology), or, "pure intuition" (metaphysical ontology) of "how earthly human comes to know "anything earthly certain" becomes the acquisition of knowledge of earthly reality as "earthly reality as intention of Human Nature interacting intelligently with Nature Nature in cognitive order of qualify absolute intended actuality," (epistemological Idealism), as opposed to an "earthly reality as intended by the knower merely knowing an "anything uncertain earthly reality," (epistemological realism). The everlasting phenomenologically epistemological question still remains____ "how does earthly human come to know an actuality of existence, actuality, and, actual essence of existence?!" Within proclivity of scientific ontology, sense experience and sense perception enable human organ brain to become "a public sphere earthly reality information processor;" whereas within proclivity of metaphysical ontology Human Mind Life enables Abstract Intellect intellect to recognize, to realize, to validate "absolute necessary knowledge" of actual existence, actuality of something certain, and actuality of essence of existence. The central branch of metaphysics is ontology which is an investigation into the nature of reality (existence), actuality (being), and ultimate possibility (essence).

Ontological Argument is a metaphysical study as based upon "a priori" argument for the existence of God, asserting that the concept of the possibility of a perfect being implies existence beyond the existence of Human Nature. The two earthly reality informational synthetic propositions, "There is a God," There is no God," will everlastingly remain synthetic because neither statement can be earthly reality proven by science.

Opinion exists as a personal idiosyncratic perceptual mental perception of an observed earthly reality existing in a situational context within a given time in space in earthly reality, which personal idiosyncratic mental perception does not validate with innately "a priori" Human Mind Life knowledge in cognitive order to adequately substantiate cognitive comprehensive understanding of "in the moment" perceptual mental perception.

Paradigm, philosophically, might be defined as a "theoretical framework" upon which a theory can be built. *Paradigm* in ancient Greece formulated language as rhetoric in oratory. Rhetoric becomes the art of prose formulated as persuasive speech used as oratory toward formulating a convincing argument. A paradigm may have not one shred of scientific value, but has been linguistically structured within such linguistic context as "to seem" "to speak" believable truth! The paradigm becomes so perceivably convincing, as it gains momentum, that its followers become so convinced that they begin to assume the posturing of "apostles" preaching the rhetoric of the "social paradigm" as if it were believable creed! At this point the paradigm takes upon itself its own earthly worldly perpetual self-righteousness. The paradigm has assumed such rhetorical force that the paradigm dominates the perceptions of earthly reality of those who have come to believe it. If the paradigm held some measure of scientific validity, the paradigm might be able to display incommensurability between earthly reality linguistic rhetoric toward human Mind Life believability. Acts of Speech, as rhetoric, demand bases within Acts of Knowledge.

Paradigmatic linguistics formulates itself within an art form of rhetoric, building Speech Acts upon dialectical antagonism opposing the multitudes of earthly human perceptions, impressions, and opinions of "what is" this earthly reality. Paradigmatic linguistics, in social order, to use persuasive language to effect and to affect the paradigm's desired resolution of presented contradictions existing in society, regardless of whether or not the contradictions may appear perceptually evident, or, may appear theoretically evident, or, just appear as unreasonable to the audience, nevertheless speak Acts of Speech in social order "to persuade" a desired socio-political outcome.

Particularity exists within perceptual mental operations due to insufficient intellectual evidence. Insufficient intellectual evidence exists as a result of "incomplete" cognitive development due to insufficient knowledge.

Passion, within mental operations, exists both sentient and intellectual. Sentiently, passion reacts behaviorally impulsively as desire, pleasure, anger void of any interaction with intellectual evidence toward consequences. Intellectually, passion manifests behaviors qualified by notions of love, fear, motivation, intention toward aesthetic and rational consequences.

Percept exists within perceptual mental operations as an immediate impression upon human Practical Intellect provoked by intentional, contextual, situational, empirical stimuli. Quality of a percept depends upon (1) quality of environment, (2) quality of sense awareness, (3) quality of practical intellect, (4) quality of ego psyche awareness, and, (5) quality of personal awareness. A percept holds both cognitive and psychological attachment to the immediate sensual impression conditioned upon and influenced by the content, the context, the situation, the motive, and intention, perceived from the sense experience. Earthly human "comes to know" the experience perceptually within value and meaning placed upon content, context, situation, motivation, and intention.

Perception exists as that status within mental operations, in which earthly human begins to acquire a sensual realization of objects, events, and other beings by means of the senses' observation of concrete-empirical stimuli, first, provoking the five senses, and then, provoking practical intellect to mentally extrapolate an impression upon Practical Intellect as quality percept based and biased upon ego psyche. Perception occurs as an immediate content and context reaction to situational and intentional stimuli of environment. Perception occurs as an initial reaction by ego psyche attempting to facilitate a worthy relationship amongst Practical Intellect, Abstract Intellect, psychological ego psyche and earthly reality. A mental impression of perception comes to exist as a synthetic perceptual proposition (a guess) formed into Practical Intellect as a primary percept_____the cognitive beginning toward discovery of truth.

Perceptual awareness exists as a status within practical intellect and within ego psyche awareness as a mental status when ego psyche awareness is attempting to function as the facilitator between that which human body substance is sense experiencing at a given time in a given space in reality with that which mind comes to conceive as concept of reality. Perceptual awareness cannot void itself of psyche awareness. There cannot exist any perceptual awareness without body. There cannot exist any perceptual awareness without psyche awareness. Perceptual awareness exists as more than just brain "sensing" the body. Immediate behavioral response to concrete-empirical stimuli in a given time in a given space in a given reality demands perceptual awareness... the awareness that psyche is merely "perceiving" reality, acquiring an immediate (non-qualitatively, cognitively sustainable) impression of reality, and, not qualitatively, cognitively, intellectually validating that reality.

Perceptual confidence exists within mental operations within Practical Intellect. Perceptual confidence relies upon sense awareness, ego psyche awareness, perceptual evidence, and common sense.

Perceptual decisions may be colloquially "named" "judgment calls"_____a guess. A perceptual decision provokes a perceptual reaction, based and biased, within the context of the situation which experiential stimulus provoked the need for the response. At that given moment in time in space in earthly reality that that perceptual decision was made, the perceptual decision did not use cognitively discernible knowledge in cognitive order to validate the perceptual decision.

Perceptual evidence exists as an imbalance amongst intellectual awareness amongst personal awareness with perceptual awareness with psychological ego psyche awareness, all, at once, interacting within earthly reality. Perceptual evidence exists in Practical Intellect as earthly reality synthetically inferred information (a guess), and, earthly reality quality of sensible intuition of sense experience forming a sense perception____a guess.

Perceptual judgment exists as perceptual mental ability within Practical Intellect mental operations based upon perceptual awareness evoking a need to validate perceptual inference by means of an observable earthly reality that can be sense experienced and sense perceived "a posteriori"_____originating as a guess.

Perlocutionary speech acts, within linguistic expression, denote a quality of emotive speaking that demonstrated the effect and/or the affect that the locutionary speech act along with the illocutionary speech act provoked upon either the emotions, thoughts, or behaviors of the listener(s) toward persuading, convincing, scaring, enlightening, inspiring "desired" social behaviors.

Performativity professes the Speech Acts can effect and affect "desired" social behaviors. If an individual "chose" not only "to believe," but, also, "to perform" according to system of secular thought and according to contemporary system of belief in science, then, he "socially and politically performed" correctly according to that which speech acts of secular thought "told" was "proper" performance. According to contemporary social science earthly human does not hold a human Mind Life, therefore earthly human cannot form a thought, however, can be persuaded to behave a social science desired social performance. Contemporary earthly human must "hear" and "listen" to Speech Acts that "tell" earthly human how "to perform" social earthly reality behaviors. Performativity exist within contemporary social science as social awareness that Speech Acts have the capacity to initiate and to consummate "desired" social behaviors, and, to even construct and perform these social behaviors as an identity in set groups.

Perspective exists as a mental operation that attempts to take public sphere information and meaningfully relate it to a content and contextual situation. Perspective does not qualify that the public sphere information may be valued as objective. Perspective uses current public sphere information as a frame of reference. Perspective comes to exist in human practical Mind Life as a "perceptual judgment." Contemporary earthly human "perspective" becomes individualized perception, impression, opinion of public sphere information.

Personal awareness exists within mental operations as "self's" mental ability to co-relate that which mental operations "know" that is stored in practical intellect with that which mental operations "know" that is stored in abstract intellect which may both reflect upon both intellects interacting with ego psyche within earthly reality, and, in reverse, which may come to cause an effect or an affect upon ego psyche interacting intellects within earthly reality. ***Personal awareness*** may tell "self" that cognitive awareness can enable conscious awareness "to come to know" earthly reality both perceptually qualitatively and conceptually qualitatively at the same time in the same space in the same earthly reality.

Phatic acts, within linguistic expression, denote a quality of emotive speaking used to express and to establish an intended behavioral impression of contemporary social science desired behavioral "sociability" amongst earthly humans rather than any attempt at imparting cognitive intellectual evidence.

Phenomena comes to exist as an immediate perceptual awareness of a situational and contextual sense experience (conscious experience) which perception of that situational and contextual sense experience provokes human Mind Life mentally operational consideration toward possibility of cognitive validation. Phenomena exists as a situational and contextual possibility happening within that which appears real to the senses but cannot necessarily be cognitively validated, either inductively inferentially or sensibly intuitively, by sense experience.

Phenomenology as a contemporary academic study holds basis and bias as a social science psychological study of earthly human conscious experience of earthly reality sense perceptions, sense impressions, sense opinions. Social science professes that current academic of phenomenology came to exist as social scientific paradigmic theories in social order to socially establish social fact standards because social science had denied the metaphysical____no standard of moral, good, or, reason; just social facts of earthly human sense perceptions, sense impressions, sense opinions of phenomenal, uncertain earthly reality. Documents It is impossible in a single earthly reality earthly human lifetime for an earthly human to come to sense experience every humankind sense experience that ever occurred. You would have to have the Mind of God! It is impossible in a single earthly reality earthly human lifetime for an earthly human to come to learn every humankind historical occurrence. And! Earthly human body substance earthly reality sense experiences are extremely limited by quality and quantity of earthly human sense experiences of earthly reality. Also! Extremely limited to earthly human quantity and quality, by virtuous reason, of an earthly humans body substance physical qualities, as well as, an earthly humans intelligence meaningful measured by cognitive development of cognitive function of the understanding. The phenomenology of experiencing a sense experience results that an earthly human can only **take a guess** what that is. **The guess** becomes a sense perception, a sense impression, or a sense opinion. As example: you witnessed on your TV that a man walked into a building. You, first hand, do not know, nor can you discern from what you witnesses who the man was, nor can you, first hand, discern that the building is, in fact, the Saudi Arabi embassy in Turkey. You do not, first hand, knew that the building is even in Turkey. You are told this earthly reality synthetic information second hand, which was probably toward second hand. You need corroboration. You are told much earthly reality synthetic information. You are shown men killing the man. Who films killing a man especially in such horrid situation. Who was there to film the killing, and, give the film to the public sphere to witness? You do not know that the killing occurred in the Saudi Arabi embassy in Turkey. Yet! You sense experience that which you witnessed; you freely willingly "believe" all that you are told as the truth. Why? Such a phenomena!

Phenotype exists with contemporary system of science that suggests that the observation of molecular biological behaviors (RNA) are physiologically represented in genotypes, and, this biological behavioral representation exists as earthly human phenotype. DNA represents an earthly human body substance, as a human species organism, molecular biological genotype. Sociology, junk science, and pharmaceutical science have taken hold of notions of human DNA (genotype) and human RNA (phenotype) and have developed "myth" telling about earthly human social diseases, about human shortcomings, suggesting and offering medical "fixes" toward that which presently ails humankind. The veracity of medical science has become dependent upon economy, earthly human lack of knowledge, and, earthly human conscience.

Philosophy, as a discipline, speculates notions of the possibility of human Mind Life metaphysical thought which might come to discover, reflect, and explain metaphysical, beyond any scientific possibility of empirical validation, principles and prototypes which could possibly "be" the essence and existence of Human Nature.

Philosophy of Language, existing within consideration given by contemporary linguistics, first (1) gives consideration to the ability of language to establish meaning based upon structure, function, and vocabulary, as well as, based within theoretical and pragmatic theories of the actuality of establishing "social truth" by means of language. Second (2) gives consideration to the use of language, as a contemporary linguistic notion, that the function of language is its "social" use in regards to social interaction, transparency, performance, discourse, and hermeneutics. Third (3) gives consideration the "social" significance to "knowing language." How does a word come to mean in regards to symbol (sign), words (vocabulary), and grammar (syntax) as formulated and used to promote "social value," not as consideration of the use of language for the acquisition of knowledge-for-the-sake-of-knowledge, but as consideration of the use of language in social order to establish "social value." Fourth (4) gives consideration to how language can come to possibly relate "social truth in earthly reality."

Philosophy of Mind, foremost, must give consideration to the notion of the everlasting ontological, metaphysical, epistemological "unresolved" question of the relationship between earthly human body substance and transcendental human Mind Life. Philosophy and theology gave speculation, and, science could not "prove," any possibility of successful interaction between human Mind Life and earthly reality, therefore, a philosophy of mind remains as speculation. Philosophy of Mind, aftermost, must give consideration to the everlasting ontological, metaphysical, epistemological "unresolved" question "does cognitive awareness and conscious awarenesses exist" within earthly human body substance as human Mind Life. Philosophy of Mind, aftermost, must give consideration to the everlasting ontological, metaphysical, epistemological "unresolved" question "within earthly human body substance does there only exist physical property and mental physical property." Philosophy of Mind, as contemporary scientific investigation, refuses to consider the phenomena of mind-reality within ontological, metaphysical, epistemological speculations, contemporary science attempting "to prove" that which cannot be "scientifically proven!" Contemporary science credits earthly human organ brain as all there is by which earthly human body substance and mental substance (human organ brain) can come to know anything as earthly reality information.

Philosophy of Science theorizes "property dualism" as consideration within a scientific philosophy of mind that suggests that within earthly reality there can exist only one kind of substance which is the "physical kind." "Physical substance contains two kinds of properties"____ physical substance properties and mental substance properties. Scientific connotation of the term "property" signifies a quality or an attribute of the physical substance, because, for contemporary science there exists no other kind of substance except the physical. Physical substance has only one quality or attribute____physical! Physical substance can change properties (states) of matter____however, these properties (states) of matter always remain physical. "Relationship" existing between physical property and mental property, since the physical property and the mental property both exist within earthly human physical substance, presents both ontological as well as logical conundrum for science. *Functionalism* is a suggested theory, using scientific method of inductive inference, toward an speculative explanation of possibility of relationship between physical property and mental property within earthly human body substance. Mental properties, functioning within earthly human organ brain matter, are conditionally provoked and stimulated by the particular sense experience and sense perception occurring at the time when a physical mental response is required. Emergence is a scientific theory of possibility of relationship between physical properties and mental properties using scientific method of "inferential induction." *Emergence theory* suggests that complex systems form patterns as a result of a multiplicity of earthly human physical interactions with earthly reality. An emergent behavior will come to stimulate behaviors, that, over the occurrence of the multiplicity of these physical interactions, come to cause "new unpredictable and irreducibly understandable" behaviors to be manifested. These newly emergent behaviors become "irreducibly understandable" to contemporary science because contemporary science may not use metaphysical, ontological, or epistemological methods of attempting "understanding!" For contemporary science "irreducible understanding" exists as earthly reality "social facts" which have been sense experienced by human body substance five senses.

Philosophical speculation comes to exist as theoretical thought using human Mind Life cognitive level of reason.

Phronesis existed for the Ancient Greeks as a metaphysical idea within philosophical speculation as *practical wisdom*. For the Ancient Greeks, phronesis was sensible intuition using practical intelligence____not using sense perception, seems impression, sense opinion gained from sense experience of earthly reality. Practical Intellect took "mental moments" in social practical and pragmatic order to discern prudent phronesis_____what to do, how to do it, in social order to cause the least harm, to achieve a common good for the most, in social order to achieve, for, the most, impartial outcome.

Polite learning is achieved when an individual acquires a reasonable intellect, an aesthetic appreciation, human respect, a moral human Mind Life, graciousness in social manner, and kindness.

Population thinking comes to exist as an "generic attitudinal" system of reality, system of truth, and system of belief that environmentally and perceptually influences earthly human thinking permeating a system of thought within general population thinking as "generic attitude." ***Generic attitude*** becomes an earthly reality perceptual, impressionable, opinionated public sphere attitude status of observed socio-political earthly reality within context of Secular Ideology within earthly reality. Secular Ideology generic attitude status tends to evoke within secular society an intellectual cognitive status of cognitive dissatisfaction and psychological dissatisfaction. Generic social secular attitude may become a perceptual expression of lack of self-conscious awareness, because earthly human neither holds significant and sufficient information about Secular Ideology, nor, significant and sufficient cognitive awareness of human Mind Life. Secular ideology generic attitude may affect the possibility toward earthly human mutual perceptual awareness about socio-political earthly reality negating any possibility of a dialectical discussion amongst earthly humans. Secular ideology generic attitude evokes cognitive and psychological status disconnect amongst earthly humans.

Carl Jung suggested two notions of ego psyche types____one as becoming extraverted "attitude," and, the other, as becoming introverted "functions" ____ego psyche may acquire an extraverted "attitude" as a perceptual status within earthly reality establishing ego psyche false over-confidence in a social secular generic attitude as a self-righteousness socio-political value____ego psyche may acquire an introverted "social functioning" when ego psyche becomes overwhelmed by the self-righteousness of extroverted "social value ego psyche's secular generic attitude." Within contemporary secular social earthly reality there exists no mutual perceptions, impressions, opinions of "what is" earthly reality. Contemporary population thinking has come to be overwhelmed to establish a secular ideology generic attitude. Generic attitude develops as the result (1) of secularization, because (2) human Mind Life in society begins to place materialistic rationalized value and meaning upon human existence in earthly reality, which comes to cause (3) "psychological disenchantment," and, "psychological evanesce" resulting in loss of (4) a moral conscience (Max Weber). Secularization becomes a societal phenomena whereby an evanesce of the collective unconsciousness (Carl Jung) of the awareness of former societal traditions, mores, and customs gradually disappear. Secularization becomes a societal phenomena whereby the effervescent, noble spirit of human kind fades away (Max Weber). Secularization replaces that effervescent, noble spirit with "a generic attitude." Secular ideology generic attitude acquires an earthly reality secular status that denies the existence of an essential human Mind Life as a personalized, individualized Human Animus____an elan vital (Henri Bergson). Human Mind Life cognitive development goes dormant. Social language development becomes limited to earthly reality socio-political vocabulary voided of any metaphysical language awareness____ such as good, kind, moral, polite, decency, integrity. Human conscious awareness of metaphysical language goes dormant. Metaphysical concert development goes dormant.

Positivism had maintained that social human behavior was best investigated by means of "quantifying" "real" "observable" social human behavior. Positivism had suggested that pre-determined, scientific, mathematical "formal" language could come to "logically" define social human behavior. Ferdinand Tonnies had suggested that the human phenomena could not be explained (understood) without using "metaphysical concepts." Both Positivism and AntiPositivism disclaimed use of philosophical, metaphysical, and epistemological language within "scientific sociological" investigation and within scientific explanation of social human behavior by formulation of "social scientific paradigms."

Possibility becomes the potentiality of coming into actuality. Possibility may come to be realized as a capability, as an earthly human Mind Life cognitive development, or, as a sublime force pro formance.

Potentiality becomes the possibility of coming into actuality. Potentiality may come to be realized as a capability, as an earthly human Mind Life cognitive development, or, as a sublime force pro formance.

Power as a force performance of human Mind Life can never be taken or be given once human Mind Life force pro formance has been gift given to Human Nature by Intelligent Design. Earthly human process of human Mind Life "thinking" about self as a self existing in an earthly reality force pro forms human Mind Life "to take control "of self as free will self-responsibility for self force pro forming in an earthly reality. Unfortunately, ***socio-cultural-political power*** in earthly reality is sensibly intuited from sense experience of phenomenal earthly reality as ***a sensibly intuited illusion*** because human Mind Life inalienable power can never be taken or given. Power exists similar to personal knowledge______I can never give you my power, or, knowledge, of my human Mind Life, and, you can never give me your power, or, knowledge, of your human Mind Life. Everyman Human Nature holds the same cognitive power potential as Everyman Human Nature cognitive power potential____regardless of any physical defect of physical human brain. Metaphysical human Mind and physical human brain processes are not equal.

Practical intellect exists within mental operations as that status of intellect when ego psyche is attempting to immediately perceptually facilitate Practical Intellect interaction with earthly reality. Ego psyche acquires initial perceptions, impressions, opinions of earthly reality by means of (1) a provocation by sense experience with concrete-empirical stimuli, (2) a psyche awareness of "self" existing within this concrete-empirical stimuli, (3) both a physiological and a psychological need to adapt to the concrete-empirical stimuli, (4) a personal awareness of present individual idiosyncratic knowledge stored in Practical Intellect as an ability to co-relate present individual idiosyncratic knowledge stored in Abstract Intellect, in order to (5) mentally reflect upon how ego psyche can interact between the two intellects interacting with earthly reality in cognitive order that both intellects can interact with ego psyche within earthly reality within an immediately required content and context situational interaction.

Pragmatic exists as practical earthly reality socio-political behaviors relying upon earthly reality public sphere information usually inferentially referencing Practical Intellect and ego psyche perceptions, impressions, and opinions of a pragmatic and practical earthly reality.

Pragmatism is a theory that suggested that theoretical evaluations could be placed into practice by means of social scientific paradigms.

Prayer exists as an esoteric virtuous practice beseeching "hope." Hope is a virtue seeking the "goodness" by reason for "something" to exist. By virtue of "somethings" existence "anything," even earthly reality uncertain, possesses "meaning" and "value" toward "some" "reason" for "something" to exist. Earthly human, in earthly human search for truth has not, yet, become capable of practice of virtue. Practice of virtue requires a very "high" level of intellectual evidence and intellectual confidence. Prayer may become a cognitive mentally operational habit of "faith" that "anything earthly" does have a virtuous reason to exist as "something" meaningful and valuable in existence.

Predilection exists within human Mind Life cognitive mental operations dependent upon quality of reasonable intellect, aesthetic intellect, quality of intellectual evidence, refinement of discernment, esoteric thought, free will, and self-responsibility.

Predisposition exists as a quality of mentally operational habit that has been qualified by the insight of intellectual evidence, or, as an earthly reality behavioral habit that has been conditioned by instinct, sensible intuition, imitation, sense perceptions of sense experiences.

Primary intellect exists in human Mind Life beginning cognitive mental operations as intellectual status of Practical Intellect when ego psyche is attempting to immediately perceptually facilitate Practical Intellect practically and pragmatically behaviorally interacting with earthly reality. Ego psyche acquires initial perceptions, impressions, opinions of earthly reality by means of (1) a provocation of sense experience with concrete-empirical stimuli, (2) ego psyche awareness of "self" existing within this concrete-empirical stimuli, (3) both a physiological and a psychological need to adapt to the concrete-empirical stimuli, (4) a personal awareness of present individual idiosyncratic knowledge stored in Practical Intellect as practical and pragmatic behavioral ability to successfully interact with earthly reality, toward wider, and, more in depth cognitive reflection upon cognitively how ego psyche can interact with earthly reality using Practical Intellect toward cognitively interacting with Abstract Intellect interacting with earthly reality in cognitive order that both intellects can interact with ego psyche within earthly reality not merely as an immediately required content and context re-actional impulsive interaction.

Primary percepts remain within Practical Intellect as immediate perceptions, impressions, opinions of sense perception of sense experience. Sense perceptions, impressions, opinions provoke Practical Intellect to react to earthly reality as an immediate, practical reaction which may not result in cognitive validation, psychological satisfaction, or cognitive satisfaction. Quality of ego psyche awareness, personal awareness, cognitive development, and conscious awareness will influence possibility of the transformation of precarious primary percepts into meaningful, valuable, absolutely necessary secondary concepts. Ego psyche awareness exists as quality of Practical Intellect's primary percepts self awareness ability to acquire perceptual awareness of "self" as existing tangibly in human body substance intangibly in human Mind Life needing to function as a quality of thought (perceptual or conceptual) either linguistically or behaviorally in a social-cultural earthly reality. Psyche awareness functions as a facilitator and as a qualifier between that which human body substance comes to sense experience as perceptions, impressions, opinions of earthly reality toward assisting human Mind Life to bring forward Abstract Intellects metaphysical concepts of the essence of earthly reality existence.

Psyche awareness comes "to realize" that "self" is a unique, personal, idiosyncratic phenomena existing within a contextual, situational environment. Personal awareness exists within human Mind Life mental operations as "self's" mental ability to co-relate that which human Mind Life mental operations "know" that is stored in Practical Intellect with that which human Mind Life mental operations "know" that is stored in Abstract Intellect which may reflect upon how both intellects interact with ego psyche within earthly reality, and, in reverse, which may come to reflect upon how ego psyche interacts using both intellects within earthly reality. Status of psyche awareness development comes to determine if ego psyche "calls upon" Abstract Intellect for assistance within human Mind Life mental operations attempting "to come to know" a necessary absolute abstract, conceptual "should be" earthly reality as opposed "to only knowing a concrete-empirical relationship (sense perception of sense experience) "what is" earthly reality.

Ego Psyche becomes the personality of an earthly human which exists in human Mind Life, intangibly, when human Mind Life, intangibly, attempts cognitive mental functions as expression of earthly human social-cultural behavior within a contextual, situational environment. Ego Psyche exists as the facilitator and a qualifier between that which human body substance sense experiences as perceptions, impressions, opinions of earthly reality, and, that which human Mind Life conceives as earthly reality. Ego Psyche functions as a unique, personal, idiosyncratic phenomena within any contextual, situational environment. Ego Psyche acts as a unique facilitator as a expression of "self" as ego psyche interacting with Practical Intellect interacting with Abstract Intellect within earthly reality.

Ego Psyche "realizes" psyche awareness that ego psyche exists uniquely alone as a persona animus phenomena in a contextual and situational relative reality. Healthy Ego Psyche, in cognitive and in social order, qualitatively, cognitively, intellectually, psychologically interact with earthly reality using human Mind Life. Healthy Ego Psyche holding psyche awareness "knows" that quality of knowledge held in Practical Intellect, and, that quality of knowledge held in Abstract Intellect establishing persona animus personal awareness of human Mind Life conscious awareness____ "knowing" how to use intellectual evidence toward earthly reality advantage.

Principles exist as essential everlasting knowledge awareness toward possibility and potentiality of Something to be the Something's "good" actuality.

Principle of Sufficient Reason, suggested by Gottfried Wilhelm Leibniz, (1646-1716), gave consideration that mathematical truths reasonably derive from the nature of their own identity. The nature of mathematical nature, of-and-by-itself, cannot contradict itself without denying itself.

Probity exists in human Mind Life as cognitive level of moral reason.

Process comes to exist as development of "nothing" *becoming "something."*

Proclivity exists as a mental bias toward a specific possibility.

Profane exists within earthly reality as pragmatic, perceptual, contextual, situational, non-qualitative earthly human expression and behavior by human Practical Intellect mental operations as human expression and human behavior non-consciously aware of essential and principled archetypes and prototypes of Human Nature, and, Human Nature necessary contingency as human Mind Life intellectual obligation and cognitive burden to be Human Nature within earthly reality. (Ruth Nanda Ashen).

Pro formations exist innately "a priori" inherent in human Mind Life. Pro formations exist in human Mind Life as the essence nature of Human Nature manifesting Human Nature into earthly reality as human Mind Life. Pro formations, innately "a priori" inherently existing in Human Mind Life are defined by the necessary principled archetypes and prototypes, which, of necessary contingency toward possibility and potentiality for Human Nature to actually exist, define Human

Nature. Plato suggested that these sublime pro formations exist as the Forms of Human Nature. Aristotle suggested that these sublime pro formations exist in satiated in earthly reality everything in cognitive order that earthly human can recognize and realize Human Nature as an actual "good" Something existing in earthly reality. Ruth Nanda Ashen suggested that Intelligent Design of these sublime pro formations, defining Human Nature, by virtue of their existence, places intellectual obligation and cognitive burden upon Human Nature to manifest the nature of Human Nature into earthly reality as an Intellectually Designed "good," "moral," and, "reasonable" Human Nature. How do you know this? Because you know it!

Profound exists as a metaphysical quality within human Mind Life mental operations within earthly human existing within earthly reality as a metaphysical conscious awareness that Human Nature exists as profoundly good, moral, and reasonable. Earthly reality, human ego psyche paying too much attention to earthly reality, and human free will____all can corrupt.

Prolegomena exists as a philosophical speculation offered by Immanuel Kant, (1724-1804), as "non de plume" toward recognition and realization of metaphysical human Mind Life essence. David Hume, (1711-1776), an Enlightenment philosopher similar to Immanuel Kant, however, while Kant held a rational worldview, Hume has become known in history for holding an empiricist philosophical worldview. Hume expressed skepticism in his philosophy that there never could be any metaphysical human Mind Life. (Author's note: Skepticism presents earthly reality with a negative worldview; a negative worldview never holds possibility of a positive rational worldview). Kant's supported his philosophical worldview by introducing into earthly human thought explanation metaphysical concepts that are worthy knowledge for earthly human to come to know. Kant introduced metaphysical concepts into earthly reality such as "knowledge a priori," knowledge a posteriori," "synthetic earthly reality propositions" never earthly reality provable because these earthly reality propositions are synthetic (guesses). Kant, similar to Georg Wilhelm Friedrich Hegel, proposed human Mind Life faculty of intelligent human ability to take a synthetic judgment (earthly reality chaos) into human Mind Life logical analytical thought and move earthly reality chaotic thought into logical, reasonable synthesis of contradictory earthly reality propositions into agreeable judgment. Immanuel Kant purposed that human Mind Life ***innately held "a priori" possibility of pure concepts that should guide earthly human.*** (Author's note: earthly human must acknowledge that which he knows, that which he does not know, that which he needs to come to know.)

Propensity exists as a mental bias directed toward a specific possibility.

Proposition exists as a linguistic "a posteriori" statement suggested toward linguistic argument or linguistic discourse seeking cognitive intellectual validation, or, intellectual invalidation by means of "a priori" human Mind Life intellectual evidence. A theory comes to exist as a synthetic proposition toward explanation by means of experiment, observation, data collecting of observable phenomena. Theoretical thought or thoughtful speculation within human Mind Life cognitive mental operations comes to exist as a quality of dynamic speculation, synthetic propositions, and/or, hypothesis, provoking scientific observation, experiment, data collecting and/or philosophically reasoned speculation. Theoretical thought or thoughtful speculation comes to provoke human Mind Life as a result of the biases recognized and realized within (1) sense perception of sense experiences, (2) earthly reality sensible intuition of synthetically inferred information, (3) perceptual evidence, (4) quality of intellectual evidence, (5) possibility and potentiality within Abstract Intellect's cognitive awareness of quality of cognitive level function of the understanding.

Prototypes exist as archetypical principles innately essential within human Mind Life recognition and realization in cognitive order to recognize and to realize Human Nature and human Mind Life.

Prototypical abstraction presents itself to human Mind Life within mental operations when mental operations can recognize and realize innate "a priori" conceptual comparative prototypes of human essential existence, and, use ***prototypical abstraction*** in cognitive order to cognitively validate intellectual evidence against earthly reality sense perceptions, sense impressions, sense opinions, perceptual evidence, earthly reality synthetic information sense inferential induction, earthly reality quality of sensible intuition, sense experience, and any sense experience occurring as conscious experience.

Provoke comes to exist within a quality of mental operations as a sense perception of a sense experience in Practical Intellect, or, as a metaphysical genesis toward metaphysical awareness in Abstract Intellect.

Psyche becomes the personality of an earthly human which exists in human Mind Life, intangibly, when human Mind Life as metaphysical existence, intangibly, attempts cognitive mental functions as earthly reality expression of social-cultural behavior within a contextual, situational environment. Psyche exists as the facilitator and the qualifier between that which human body substance sense experiences as perception, impression, opinion, and, that which human Mind Life conceives as abstract absolute concepts of earthly reality. Psyche functions as a unique, personal, idiosyncratic cognitive mental phenomena within any contextual, situational concrete environment. Quality of psyche is influenced by quality of emotion because emotion functions as a both an intellectual and a psychologically influencing mental qualifier between intellect and psyche.

Psyche, performing as perception, impression, opinion personally idiosyncratically perceives earthly reality, placing earthly reality perceptions, impressions, opinions into Practical Intellect. Psyche facilitates and mediates cognitive interaction occurring between Abstract Intellect and Practical Intellect,. Psyche, as Practical Intellect, qualifies earthly reality information in attempt tp allow Abstract Intellect to validate earthly reality information.

Quality of perceptual psyche awareness of phenomenal earthly reality____quality of psychological psyche awareness will determine believability of earthly reality information.

Psyche awareness exists within Practical Intellect mental operations as "self's" mental ability to acquire a quality of psyche awareness of "self" as existing tangibly in human body substance, and, intangibly in human Mind Life needing to cognitively function as a quality of earthly reality thought either linguistically or behaviorally in a social-cultural earthly reality. Psyche awareness functions as a facilitator and as a qualifier between that which human body substance comes to sense experience as perceptions, impressions, opinions of earthly reality, and, that which human Mind Life abstractly conceptually conceives of earthly reality. Psyche awareness comes "to recognize and to realize" that "self" is a unique, personal, idiosyncratic phenomena existing within a contextual, situational phenomenal earthly reality.

Psychology, today, exists as a science of scientific investigation of human body substance existing as human organ brain and five senses interacting within earthly reality as physical property and as physical mental property, by happenstance, sense experiencing a conscious experience. Psychology, of old, was a discipline under philosophical study, and, was a study into the nous and the animus of Human Nature. When modern science decided that earthly human did not have either nous or animus, modern psychology void study of human Mind Life, human ego psyche, nou and human animus____but____earthly human did not.

Psychological awareness exists within human Mind Life cognitive mental operations as awarenesses of psyche awareness interaction with personal awareness, intellectual awareness, and conscious awareness.

Psychological bias exists within human Mind Life cognitive mental operations first as a status within psychological qualification toward psychological reflection toward psychological resolution.

Psychological confidence exists within human Mind Life cognitive mental operations when ego psyche recognizes and realizes that ego

psyche can interact with human body substance sense experiences
as psyche awareness, perceptual awareness, perceptual evidence, and
perceptual judgment successfully with personal awareness, cognitive
awareness, intellectual evidence, and conscious awareness.

Psychological development becomes human Mind Life earthly reality
phenomena of psyche awareness. Psychological development becomes
human Mind Life persona phenomena developing as the result of
an earthly human personalized idiosyncratic cognition interacting
within an earthly human ego psyche awareness within a phenomenal
earthly reality. Human Mind Life psychological development brings
into earthly reality existence "a one-and-only" psyche awareness____
coming to exist as a unique earthly reality persona animus____an elan
vital. Psychological development brings forth the "challenge" of earthly
human existence____toward a quality of intellectual development,
toward a quality of psyche awareness, toward a quality of human Mind
Life conscious awareness interacting with ego psyche awareness within
phenomena of earthly reality.

Psychological disequilibrium exists when one of the two factors of
psychological equilibrium, intellect and psyche, are not in balance
with each other, when one of the two factors overwhelms the other.
Psychological disequilibrium will cause a status of awareness as a self-
consciousness. Intellect and psyche remain in a state of imbalance within
phenomenal earthly reality.

Psychological dissatisfaction exists within human Mind Life cognitive
mental operations as a status of self-consciousness.

Psychological equilibrium exists within human Mind Life cognitive
mental operations as ability toward establishing a balance between
intellect and psyche within phenomenal earthly reality. Psychological
equilibrium remains within in a state of dynamic flux cognitive
adaptation. Psychological equilibrium requires cognitive equilibrium as
validation.

Psychological perception exists within human Mind Life cognitive mental operations as limited psychological awareness because of inadequate personal awareness, and, because of conscious awareness of only Practical Intellect, and, because of no cognitive interaction with intellectual awareness. Ego Psyche relying upon psychological perception limits eg psyche quality interactions within phenomenal earthly reality because ego psyche "perceives" phenomena earthly reality limited to conscious experience between Practical Intellect and phenomenal earthly reality. Behavioral, or, quality of mental interaction between ego psyche and earthly reality relying upon a status of psychological perception instead of relying upon human Mind Life intellectual evidence severely limits human Mind Life intellectual conscious awareness interacting within earthly reality.

Psychological awareness quality within human Mind Life cognitive awareness of psyche awareness qualifies, facilitates, and mediates cognitive interaction with personal awareness, intellectual awareness, and conscious awareness. Human Mind Life mental operational ability of psychological awareness intervenes with personal awareness, intellectual awareness, and conscious awareness within human Mind Life mentally operational processes of reflection, discernment, and cognitive resolution of contradictions arising between ego psyche and intellects in cognitive order to force pro form a cognitive judgment about the possibility of a meaningful interaction amongst intellects interacting with ego psyche interacting within earthly reality. Psyche awareness use of perceptual, practical, pragmatic mental operations within psychological perceptions limits psyche awareness interaction with earthly reality to an "egotistical perception" of earthly reality that exists more as perceptual awareness than as intellectual awareness. Psyche awareness relies on egotistical perception. Egotistical perception deceives!

Psychological qualification exists as a mental operational status existing in human Mind Life as ego psyche. Ego psyche egotistical awareness demands cognitive mental considerations toward psychological reservation of psychological expectations which are limiting the possibility of the recognition and the realization of essential true knowledge of ontological truth innately held as Human Nature attributes and characteristics toward nourishing actuality of human Mind Life purpose.

Psychological realization comes to exist as a cognitive mental ability within human Mind Life as a cognitive recognition between psyche awareness and intellectual awareness. Plato suggested that intellectual awareness exists as good conscious awareness whereas ego psyche "blurs" good-in-common limited by "good-in-selfish."

When human Mind Life intellectual awareness comes to mediate psyche awareness "toward recognition and realization of "good-in-common" the result becomes psychological satisfaction within human Mind Life.

Psychological reflection exists as human Mind Life mental consideration that enables psyche awareness to contemplate cognitive awareness with conscious awareness in cognitive order to consider a possibility toward psychological resolution as "good-in-common."

Psychological reflection provokes ego psyche to interact with intellects, both intellects existing as cognitive awareness and conscious awareness, in an attempt to qualify psychological reservations and psychological expectations which are limiting recognition of human Mind Life essential attributes of teleological purposeful functions as nourishing characteristics of intellectual conscious awareness amongst ego psyche interacting with human Mind Life intellectual evidence interacting within earthly reality. Process of psychological qualification may manifest interaction between ego psyche and both intellects within several status of reflection: (1) psychological transference, (2) psychological disequilibrium, (3) psychological dissatisfaction, (4) rationalization, (5) psychological bias, (6) self-consciousness, (7) psychological equilibrium, (8) psychological satisfaction, (9) psychological resolution.

Psychological resolution encompasses the use of cognitive awareness with conscious awareness toward any realization of just how intellectual evidence comes to influence ego psyche, and, in reverse, just how ego psyche comes "to blur" intellectual evidence____toward ontological psychological reflective qualification toward teleological psychological and intellectual resolution.

Psychological satisfaction exists within human Mind Life mental operations as quality good psychological realization that human Mind Life intellectual evidence has force pro formed perceptual awareness into intellectual awareness. When intellectual awareness overwhelms ego psyche perceptions cognitive result is a psychological satisfaction. Psychological satisfaction may be influenced by emotion. Emotion is a quality within mental operations by means of which human Mind Life discerns the value of organizational, categorical ordering of the acquisition of new knowledge validated with existing knowledge toward acquiring a personal idiosyncratic system of reality, system of truth, and system of belief. Emotion may have a positive or a non-positive effecting and affecting influence upon cognitive mental operations as earthly reality consequences since obligation and burden of emotional intelligence influences quality of psyche awareness.

Psychological transference will occur due to both intellectual and psychological void in human Mind Life. Psychological transference occurs as ego psyche attempting to validate ego psyche when ego psyche does not seek the intellectual evidence within human Mind Life. Quality of ego psyche awareness attempts to validate ego psyche behavior with past or present quality of inadequate ego psyche awareness.

Purposeful psychological consequence comes to exist within status of human Mind Life mental operations when cognitive mental operations establish a new conscious awareness that balances cognitive equilibrium with psychological equilibrium, and, balances cognitive satisfaction with psychological satisfaction.

Qualify exists within human Mind Life mental operations when either practical intellect or abstract intellect attempt a status of cognitive validation enabling value or significance to be given to the experience.

Quality is a word, in the context of this manuscript, which connotes a degree of excellence.

Quantity is a word, in the context of this manuscript, which connotes a degree of amount.

Reactionary impulsiveness was a notion suggested by Franz Boas, (1858-1942). Boas speculated that human Mind Life develops reactionary impulsiveness toward stimuli that cause human Mind Life to develop earthly reality behavioral habits to become less consciously aware with that which intellects interacting with ego psyche interacting with earthly reality are doing. Reactionary impulses are immediate behavioral reactions driven by instinct, or imitation, or perceptual inferences void of any intellectual evidence toward behavioral response to immediate contextual, situational, relative reality that cause certain behavioral reactions to effect and to affect unfavorable consequences. Reactionary impulsiveness (Boas) exists as a subjective inferential of a contextual, situational, immediate sense perception of a sense experience coming to exist momentarily in abeyance of intellectual evidence within human Mind Life. Human Mind Life intellectual evidence in abeyance will not permit an intellectual judgment rather an immediate reactionary impulse.

Reality is that existence which exists outside of earthly human. Earthly reality exists as an earthly human personal, idiosyncratic system of reality, system of truth, and system of belief.

Realize, as defined within Human Mind Life mental operations, becomes that process within human Mind Life mental operations in which earthly human acquires cognitive developmental human Mind Life cognitive developmental functions as concept development, thought development, language development, psychological development, as well as, multiple mental awarenesses, as well as, a quality of metaphysical thought. Realize, within human Mind Life mental operations, becomes a "know self" as both intellects (Practical and Abstract Intellects) alongside ego psyche interacting within earthly reality.

Reason exists psychologically inherent, and, intellectually innately "a priori" within human Mind Life as a conscious awareness of reason existing within earthly reality.

Reason exists as human Mind Life conscious awareness of interconnectedness of abstract cognitive balance amongst intellects (Practical and Abstract Intellects), ego psyche, and earthly reality. Reason has that possibility of human Mind Life mental operation to actualize the essence of earthly human existing as an innate human Mind Life mentally operational faculty "a priori" that can abstractly "recognize and realize" the essence of right and wrong from the perceived existence of events, objects, and other earthly humans. Reason predicates human Mind Life to organize categorization classification of innate "a priori" necessarily contingent absolute universal essences of actual existence within earthly reality in cognitive order for earthly human to come to know "Something Certain as its Something Certain." Reason, in cognitive order, recognizes and realizes cognitive discernment between earthly reality good and evil. Evil exists as the absence of good. Any quality of cognitive level of the understanding may initiate the "realization" of reason. Thinking, functioning innately "a priori" within human Mind Life functions as cognitive ability to recognize and to realize reason within cognitive development. In actuality of earthly reality reason cannot be linguistically or behaviorally defined; reason exists innately "a priori" metaphysically in human Mind Life. Human Mind Life came with innate "a priori" cognitive ability to reason moral. Reason can only be metaphysically recognized and realized. Cognitive ability to manifest reason within earthly reality demands non-subjectivity (ego psyche placed in abeyance) within linguistic and behavioral expression.

Reason cognitively discerns, within human Mind Life, cognitive mental ability to intellectually develop cognitive ability to observe earthly reality nature as earthly reality nature capable of "making sense" of the interaction occurring between self and earthly reality. Reason becomes human Mind Life mentally operational provocation that cognitively evokes "self" to come to reasonably morally know earthly reality in cognitive order to establish a dynamic homeostatic relationship existing between self and earthly reality. Reason, innately existing in human Mind Life mental operations of a "for certain moral" quality of cognitive development, relies upon the epistemology of knowledge, the ontology of being, and the metaphysical mental abilities within human Mind Life innately "a priori" enabling cognitive understanding of concepts such as "being," "time," "space," "substance," "cause and effect," "first principles" in cognitive order to acquire sagacious and ingenious understanding of human Mind Life cognitively acquired moral mental awarenesses. The cognitive functional level of cognitive *reason* held innately in human Mind Life enables human Mind Life to recognize and to realize absolute necessary concept of *moral___*enabling earthly human to understand the ontology and the teleology of Human Nature existing within earthly reality.

Earthly reality corrupts Human Nature existing as earthly human___ however, human Mind Life understanding of reason and of moral will not permit earthly reality to corrupt Human Nature. Human Nature existing as earthly human within earthly reality becomes metaphysically, esoterically wise. The nature of Human Nature existing as earthly human within earthly reality "exists to become wise."

Reason and Science remain at odds with each other's methods of acquiring awareness of being. Existence within an earthly reality. Reason, as attempting an ontological and teleological metaphysics of human Mind Life, attempts cognitive development of human Mind Life; Modern Science, as relying upon sense perception of human body substance sense perception, desires control of. Human body substance brain by means of behavioral conditioning, medicinally altering drugs, neurological stimulation, genetic alteration, psychological evaluation, societal indoctrination, and AI machines. Reason recognizes and realizes human Mind Life as an intangible force; Modern Science accepts human body substance organ brain as a physical, neurological human body substance organ that exists in a human body substance in social order for earthly human to practically, pragmatically, sensibly function within earthly reality. Reason speculates that the ontology and the teleology of human Mind Life "can come to metaphysically know" by acquiring knowledge and by means of cognitive development arriving at the cognitive development of reason. Modern Science has established that human body substance organ brain acquires earthly reality information by means of sense perception of sense experience sent by means of human body substance neurotransmitters to human body substance brain, and, modern science speculates upon just how earthly reality information "comes to be physically known" by earthly human.

Rectitude exists in human Mind Life as cognitive level of moral reason.

Recognition, as defined within human Mind Life mental operations, exists as that process within human Mind Life mental operations by which earthly human comes to perceptually identify that which exists in human Mind Life as existing within earthly reality.

Reflection is a mental ability within mental operations which enables cognitive structure and cognitive functions to mentally consider their abilities and operations in cognitive order to achieve a resolution of cognitive validation. Reflection exists as a human Mind Life cognitive function within human Mind Life mental operations which enables cognitive structure and cognitive functions to consider present knowledge in cognitive order to achieve a resolution of cognitive validation____that that which is perceived as earthly real can be cognitively validated as earthly actual. Human Mind Life mental operations demand conscious awareness of cognitive processes of thinking. The product of cognitive thinking becomes earthly human Practical and Abstract Intellects. Metaphysical thinking is the use of intellects.

Relativity. Theory of Relativity (Einstein) suggests that any measure of time necessarily becomes relatively relational to any measure of space within earthly reality. Time in space exists relative to each other. Space in time exists relative to each other. Energy is a given. Time is a conventional measurement of earthly reality in social and in cognitive order to relatively relate to changes in measurement of space.

Ontological and teleological relative changes in time and in space depend upon matter and energy. Energy changes space in time. Human perception relatively relates to time and to space. Energy is a given. The only given in the equation is energy. Energy cannot be created nor destroyed by earthly human. Time is relatively relational to space. Space is relatively relational to time. Time changes space. Space changes time. Energy is a given. Earthly human idiosyncratic perception of the sense experiences of time and of space cause time and space to exist relative to each other. Energy is a given. Earthly human can procreate new matter (space) in time with the energy that earthly human has been given____as energy work. Earthly human cannot create nor destroy energy. Energy is a given.

Is a gift a given?

Resolution exists as human Mind Life mental processes that becomes an intellectual cognitive process attempting to validate and to coalesce what sense perception of sense experience brings forth as perceptual evidence with that which Abstract Intellect knows innately "a priori" in human Mind Life. Human Mind Life cognitively functions, as resolution, using intellectual evidence in Abstract Intellect in cognitive order to bring forth renewed meaningful measure of renewed human Mind Life conscious awareness.

Responsible consequence comes to exist within human Mind Life mental status as cognitive equilibrium, cognitive satisfaction, psychological equilibrium, and psychological satisfaction when Practical Intellect alongside Abstract Intellect, using human Mind Life intellectual evidence, interacts with ego psyche interacting with earthly reality. Mattterful consequence may result as "an unintended consequence" due to ego psyche free will choosing not interact with Abstract Intellect.

Responsibility, ***Intellectual responsibility***, exists within human Mind Life mental operations by which an earthly human can intellectually, by means of cognitive awareness, conscious awareness, conscience, and knowledge, recognize and realize interaction occurring amongst intellects, ego psyche, and earthly reality.

Rhetoric, within earthly reality informational linguistic expression, exists as earthly human "speak" as perceptual awareness quality of earthly reality information specific perceptual awareness____specific perceptual awareness, within a situational context and content vocabulary selection in social oder to persuade a specific situational earthly reality content and context in social order to use specific language to effectively and to affectively influence and persuade intentional earthly reality specific thought upon the audience. Within public sphere rhetorical situational content and context usually there exists no truth value.

Sacred exists as human Mind Life metaphysical quality cognitive mental operations that seek both mysterious and profound ecumenical, often named word esoteric, awareness.

Sagacious, within human Mind Life mental operations, is achieved when earthly human acquires sufficient knowledge and acumen in discernment of human Mind Life believed, intellectually validated knowledge in cognitive order to (1) acquire knowledge-for-the-sake-of-knowledge, (2) "worthily" use of believed, intellectually validated knowledge, (3) will to use believed, intellectually validated knowledge, and, (3) take self-responsibility for human Mind Life believed, intellectually validated knowledge, and, earthly reality use of believed, intellectually validated knowledge. Knowledge-for-the-sake of knowledge itself holds no earthly reality perceptions, impressions, or, opinions. Knowledge-for-the-sake-of-knowledge is never earthly reality corrupted by earthly reality synthetic information, earthly reality perception, impression, opinion, perceptual awareness, ego psyche awareness, earthly reality bias sensible intuition, sensible intuited (guessed) inferential induction, animal instinct.

Schemas are mentally intellectually verified structured concept clusters of relational abstract absolute concepts which have been mentally operationally organized by means of categorizing commonalities and principles which could mentally meaningfully represent events, objects, and other earthly humans which have been only sense experienced as human body substance quality of mere sense perception, sense impression, sense opinion. Earthly human, "coming to know," earthly reality via Practical Intellect, as a quality of selfish ego psyche, becomes sense experienced about earthly reality as quality sense experience of perception, impression, opinion _____which quality of sense experience as perception, impression, opinion earthly reality changes earthly space in earthly time moment by moment. Human body substance of earthly reality information changes perceptual awareness moment by moment in earthly time in earthly space. Knowledge-for-the-sake-of-knowledge, of and by itself, remains as everlasting schema unless human Mind Life enriches and enhances metaphysical knowledge by renewing conscious awareness of human Mind Life's intellectual evidence.

Scholasticism existed as a system of reality, a system of truth, and a system of belief beginning in the medieval Catholic monasteries in Europe. Scholasticism held to system of reality, truth, and belief originally brought forth by the Greek philosophers that "truth" could be discovered by virtue of human Mind Life cognitive ability to reason innate "a priori" ideas, "gifts given" as prototypical archetypes, to human Mind Life, which enabled earthly human "to come to know truth."

Science, as a discipline of academic study, exists as an academic study of natural and empirical earthly reality by means of formulating theoretical hypothesis of the observation and experimentation of that natural empirical earthly reality.

Science evolved as practice of investigation into the nature, structures, and functions of human organism, existing both mentally and physically, and, as investigation into the observed universe as existing as a natural systematic natural ordering, toward an intention of discovery of the nature, structures, and functions of that natural ordering toward a determination of how a human species' phenomenally interacts with the phenomena of the natural universe that could come to result as homeostatic interaction. During Classical Greek and Roman antiquity investigation into the nature of the human Mind Life ability to acquire Nature Nature and Human Nature knowledge was considered as science. Scientia in Latin means "knowledge." Science, during classical Greece and Rome, was practiced as metaphysical science. Classical human Mind Life was both scientifically and philosophically respected. Classical science regarded human Mind Life as having ability to acquire knowledge by means of cognitive reason deduction. Human Mind Life observed human and natural phenomena, and, came to deduce by means of human Mind Life ability to cognitively reason, the nature, structures, and functions of human metaphysical Mind Life interacting within a realm of physical universe. Classical metaphysical science relied upon human Mind Life in cognitive order to discern some believable knowledge of that which human Mind Life observed and experienced. Classical science, during the Age of the Enlightenment, came to evolve as a recognition and a realization that it was human Mind Life that made the "final judgment call" about believable knowledge human Mind Life acquired as reasonably believable from science's observations and experiences about earthly reality and universe. Nevertheless, earthly human physical observation, instrumentation, and experiment could come to greatly assist human Mind Life towards human Mind Life quest for believable knowledge. Human Mind Life, based upon nature knowledge human Mind Life had acquired within genres, genre studies labeled as mathematical science, physical science, natural science, alchemy, astrology, astronomy, botany, chemistry, physics, physiology, medicine, developed instruments to assist human Mind Life in human Mind Life quest for truth knowledge. In the beginning____in the cradle of science____it was human Mind Life that brought forth knowledge of Human Nature and Nature Nature. Human Mind Life invented the instruments, diagrams, maps, mathematical algorithms, paradigms, models, hypotheses of theories, logical reasoning, and language that assisted human Mind Life as multitudes of genres investigating, within scientific practice toward "discovery" of valuable and validated knowledge of Human Nature and Nature Nature. In the beginning____ in the cradle of science____science was considered as an investigative speculation within the possibility of the existence of human Mind Life cognitive ability of deductive reasoning toward possibility of acquiring believable knowledge. Needless to say classical science remained as a philosophic approach toward acquisition of knowledge.

Science's dilemma. By modern science professing that earthly human is capable of only coming to know by human body substance behavioral impulsive reactions toward earthly reality by means of human body substance sense perceptions of sense experiences, system of belief in science becomes "confounded" by metaphysical unpredictable consequences which modern science refuses to metaphysically discern.

Scientific method refers to a scientific procedural course of action needed to scientifically systematically occur in scientific order to use an empirical method, as adverse to human Mind Life cognitive ability to deductively reason, as investigation toward acquisition of truth knowledge. Empirical method relies upon observation of existing earthly reality, and, not upon "conjecture" imposed upon earthly reality that might occur as a result of a human Mind Life mental operation called "reason." Empirical method relies upon observation, measurement, and experimentation within earthly reality. Scientific method relies upon the iterations, recursions, and orderings of (1) observations, measurements, and experiments, (2) hypotheses, even though theoretically based and biased, (3) predictions, even though using pre-specified scientifically defined logical, mathematical, or analytical propositions toward inductive and deductive conclusion, as well as "inferential induction" of observed data, and (4) conclusions, even though open to falsifiability by means of another theoretical contradictory hypothesis.

Science and Reason remain at odds with each other's methods of acquiring awareness of essence of existence. Reason, attempting a metaphysics of human Mind Life, attempts cognitive development of human Mind Life. Modern Science, as relying upon sense experience and sense perception, desires control of human body substance organ brain by means of behavioral conditioning, medicinally altering drugs, neurological stimulation, genetic alteration, psychological evaluation, societal indoctrination, an, AI machines. Reason recognizes its innate Human Nature____intelligently designed human Mind Life as an intangible force pro formance within earthly reality. Modern Science accepts human body substance organ brain as a physical, neurological human body substance organ that exists for ontological, teleological, and physiological evolutional intent "to come to know" what? Reason metaphysically speculates that human Mind Life "can come to know" by acquiring knowledge and by means of cognitive development toward the cognitive development of reason. Modern Science has established that human body substance organ brain acquires earthly reality information by means of sense perceptions of human body substance sense experiences sent by means of neurotransmitters to human body substance organ brain. Modern science scientifically speculates upon just how earthly reality information "comes to be **truthfully** known" by human body substance organ brain.

Self-centered describes an earthly human earthly-centered egotistically seeking self-gratification from earthly reality physical realm.

Secondary concepts are those abstractions human Mind Life recognizes and realizes after the aid from any concrete-empirical earthly reality sense experience. Secondary concepts are built upon human Practical Intellect primary invalidated percepts which earthly human Practical Intellect has acquired and stored into Practical Intellect. As quality of earthly reality perceptions, impressions, opinions. Secondary concepts are those abstract absolute innate "a priori" concepts whose abstract, criterial qualities yield essential meaning toward metaphysical conceptual possibility of "spirit ideas" of the actuality of the existence of an event, or, of an object, or, of another earthly human____especially secondary concept awareness by human Mind Life of universal Human Nature. All earthly humans hold the same Human Nature.

Sense perception, existing as a percept, greatly comes to influence the idiosyncrasies of the secondary concept because ego psyche not only interacts as a facilitator amongst ego psyche earthly reality psychological perception, intellects, and earthly reality____but acts as a qualifier as well___thus influencing the quality of the "spirit idea" "a priori" held by human Mind Life. From the beginning of the transcendental transformation of "a posteriori" primary percepts held in Practical Intellect to quality transformation as "a priori" secondary concepts held in Abstract Mind Life, earthly reality propositions change qualities of ability to truthfully know these earthly reality propositions. Earthly reality propositions first exists as synthetic "a posteriori" primary perceptual impressions and opinions, then, second, move toward synthetic "a priori" propositions awaiting validation from human Mind Life, then move into "a priori" quality of validated intellectual evidence.

A secondary concept will be influenced (1) by the quality of the sense experience of the quality of the environment or of the quality of the earthly reality information, (2) by the quality of the percept of the quality of the environment or of the quality of percept of the earthly reality information, (3) by the essence and the existence of an earthly human quality of cognitive status of mental operations existing within Practical Intellect interacting ego psyche awareness interacting with earthly reality, (4) by psyche awareness, (5) by personal awareness, (6) by self-awareness, (7) by intellectual awareness, (8) by conscious awareness, (9) by psychological awareness, (10) by cognitive validation, (11) by quantity and quality of knowledge, and (12) by psychological resolution all at any given mental moment in which earthly human is capable, after stimulation from concrete-empirical observational earthly reality experience, to transcendently transform the percept of the experience into the concept of the knowledge truth of the human body substance sense experience. Secondary concepts represent to human Mind Life metaphysical unpredictable consequences of contradictions existing between that which primary intellect "knows" as earthly reality___really uncertain, and, that which abstract intellect "knows" as metaphysical conceptual comparative prototypes and archetypes of existence, actuality, and essence of existence. Secondary concepts come to exist in abstract intellect as metaphysical spirit ideas.

Secularism, as a theory of epistemology, agrees with empiricism, that authoritative knowledge (believably true) can only be acquired from sense experience and sense perception, however, secularism, existing in earthly reality, as a social "ism" takes on more "socio-cultural-political" connotation than it does "scientific method," or, philosophical peculation. Secularism, as theory of societal epistemology, exists as a "social scientific paradigm." Secularism exists as an epistemological theory that the nature, sources, and limits of acquisition of knowledge become directly related to that which social, non-religious, non-ontologically social interaction comes to inform earthly human about himself interacting in a secular society. Epistemology of ideology of Secularism practices an earthly realty realm earthly-centered, self-centered void of metaphysical respect for the mysteriously sacred autonomy of Human Nature.

Secular thought exists within a quality of sociocentric thought within a possibility of two realms of the possibility of collective thought: (1) the quality of the thought of the individual contributing to (2) the collective thought within the population thinking, which population thinking "assumes" a quality of thought based and biased within social, political, and economic desalination and disenfranchisement in attempt to segregate "those who think progressively" from "those who think traditionally." "Those who think traditionally" have socially, politically, and economically desalinated and disenfranchised a segment of the population due to their system of reality, system of truth, and system of belief. "Those who think traditionally" "believe" (1) the individual holds self-responsibility and full potential of intellect and production as "free" "to become" that which he "intends" to become, (2) the individual "agrees "to play respectful" by the rules of the interplay of a "free" social, political, and economic society, (3) the individual "agrees" to interact within a standard of respect for all within a deportment of "politeness," and, (3) the individual "agrees" "to behave" ethically and morally within the societies established system of reality, system of truth, and system of belief. Western Traditional system of reality, system of truth, and system of belief "believes" in polite learning, respect for others, and Intelligent Design. Secular thought "believes" "anything" that "opposes" traditional thought about the possibility of a humane society.

"Seems" refers to "how" an earthly human, using human body substance five senses, perceives earthly reality.

Self-awareness becomes a quality of a mental operational ability to "recognize and to realize" individual, personal, idiosyncratic self-knowledge of one's individual reservoir of knowledge, of personal awareness, of intellectual awareness, of psyche awareness, and of psychological awareness in social order to cognitively "realize" a quality of psychological satisfaction and cognitive intelligence upon that self-awareness.

Self-consciousness exists within mental operations as a status of psychological dissatisfaction. When emotion, as a quality of human Mind Life cognitive mental operations, is unable to have a positive effecting or affecting influence upon a quality of ego psyche, psychological dissatisfaction may result. This qualitative status of ego psyche, when ego psyche overwhelms Practical Intellect, when Practical Intellect and ego psyche, when ego psyche and Practical Intellect, are not able to influence each other within a qualitative status of equilibrium, or "even reciprocal influence," "self" becomes aware of "self" as a conscious awareness existing within a status of disequilibrium, thus becoming more aware of self "attempting" some quality of awareness.

Self-responsibility exists by virtue of ontological and epistemological authority to exist, as that "spirit idea" of "inalienable right." Webster's definition of the word "inalienable" exist by "connotation" as "something" that cannot be transferred. Webster's definition of the word "inalienable" exist by "denotation" as "something" that can not be denied. If human holds existence, and, that ontological existence defines itself as inalienable, possessing rights of life, liberty, and happiness, then who or what, ontologically or epistemologically, becomes "responsible" for insuring earthly human "inalienable rights." "Something" called society, "something" called government, "something" called science, "something" called religion? If the "right" exists as "inalienable," a human cannot transfer his "right" to "something" else, and, the "right" of the human cannot be "denied" by "something" else, which, results in ontological and epistemological resolution that the "inalienable right" exists as the "self-responsibility" of earthly human. EVERY RIGHT ONTOLOGICALLY AND EPISTEMOLOGICALLY PRESUMES A RESPONSIBILITY! If in the case earthly human relinquishes his "self-responsibility" to a mandate of law, or to a mandate of creed, or to a theory of science, or, to a socio-political ideology, the human relinquishes his "right!" _____to do good, to behave good, to take self-responsibility.

Semantics is the consideration of "how a word comes to mean?" In contemporary cognitive science, cognitive linguistics, neurolinguistics, pragmatism, positivism, and, within social scientific paradigms, semantics became a consideration of relationship between signs and symbols and how these signs and symbols "came to signify meaning," whether as personal meaning, or, as interpersonal meaningful communication, or as hermeneutical interpretation, without any consideration of relationship of thought to language or language to thought___only as a consideration of language structure to ideology of language as socio-cultural-political meaning. Language exists as a conventionally agreed upon symbol (sign) system established as words (vocabulary) and grammar (syntax). Language, void of thought, is made up of concrete-empirical stimuli. Language as a concrete-empirical stimulus provokes "the Sense Heard or Seen" to react to "something!" Language, existing as concrete-empirical stimuli, does not possess any "meaning" other than as defining itself as a language. Concrete-empirical signs and symbols do not "mean" anything, other than that they represent a language. Language does not give meaning to thought, thought gives meaning to language. Language does not morph, thought morphs. Thought develops then language develops. Conventional language enters human Mind Life as a "synthetic a posteriori" proposition, which "synthetic a posteriori" (perceptual) proposition must "transcendently transform" into a "synthetic a priori" proposition (psyche holding percept in abeyance) until Abstract Intellect can cognitively validate the percept with "a priori" knowledge intellectually transforming the percept into a metaphysical absolute concept. Language existed first (1) as a concrete stimulus, which, (2) by means of sense experience, hearing or seeing, provoked a synthetic "a posteriori" impression upon ego psyche, then, (3) ego psyche needed to cognitively validate the synthetic "a posteriori" impression (existing as perceptual evidence of a perception or a hermeneutical interpretation) with "a priori" thought via a process of thinking using existing intellectual evidence. Thought, whether language in-or-out, always existed as language, which both, thought and language, had been personally, idiosyncratically "acquired." Language does not give meaning to thought, language acts as a "demiurge," an artificer of the world, enabling thought to acquire and to express human Mind Life metaphysical awareness. Thought develops and language develops, not necessary complimentary to each other. At some "mental moments" the child begins to realize that the the "word" chair" merely "signs" the "object" "chair." The "word" "chair" is its own entity, and, the "object" "chair" is its own entity. Within the child's cognitive development the child begins to distinguish between "words" and "objects." Concept development may not begin until the child learns to read in cognitive order to learn. When a child learns to read in cognitive order to learn the child must acquire concept awareness within the child's cognitive developmental awareness. When the child learns to read in cognitive order to learn, the child develops the first cognitive mental operation of the abstracting process. Up to that point when the child has not learned to read to learn the child's sense perceptions of his sense experiences have severely limited his acquisition of knowledge. Once the child learns to read to learn his knowledge acquisition becomes limited only to the amount of books he reads. A book can reveal to the child life experiences which the child may never physically be enabled to experience. A percept of reality held within Practical Intellect severely limits the child's learning potential___whereas a book opens human Mind Life to abstract absolute concepts and intellectual interaction with concepts which life experience may never afford. Moreover concepts abstracted from a book greatly enhance the child's perception of his life experiences. "How a word comes to mean" for the child becomes limited to his knowledge acquisition, and, not dependent upon his sense perception of his limited life experiences.

Semiotics is the consideration of the transmission, reception, and possible meaning of signs and symbols. If, even science and social scientific paradigms "assume" (admit) that everything has "some intended" meaning, then, how can it "be" that concrete-empirical signs and concrete-empirical symbols came to acquire meaning? Answer: concrete-empirical signs and concrete-empirical symbols came to acquire meaning because that meaning had been bestowed upon them by abstract thought. Abstract thought came to give significance to these concrete-empirical signs and concrete-empirical symbols. Since thought becomes personal and idiosyncratic to each earthly human, inter-personal transmission and reception of meaning becomes extremely difficult. While the signs and symbols remain the same, thought does not. Earthly human sense perceptions, sense impressions, sense opinions rarely earthly-centered agree with each other.

Sense awareness is initialized by physical body substance five senses: sight, sound, smell, taste, and touch. Sense awareness is experienced by physical body substance five senses. Sense awareness, as a physical stimulation, holds no human intellectual meaning without transforming into some quality of human Mind Life mental operations or ego psyche awareness of that which has been sense experienced. Sense perception initiates human Mind Life mental operations. A quality of cognitive awareness and psyche awareness will influence quality of sense awareness.

Sense experience occurs when one or more of human body substance five senses____sense experiences an object, event, or, other earthly humans in earthly reality sense experiences. Earthly human body substance sense experiences earthly reality causing earthly human body substance to experience a "conscious experience."

Sense perception occurs as an immediate content and context reaction to situational and intentional earthly reality stimuli; whereas conceptualization requires human Mind Life mental abstraction to be derived from empirical observation and sense experience, first transformed into an abstract primary percept, as a perception, an impression, an opinion of earthly reality, placed into Practical Intellect as a primary synthetic "a posteriori" proposition, then, transformed into synthetic "a priori" secondary concept, in human Mind Life, awaiting Abstract Intellect validation from intellectual evidence held innately "a priori" in human Mind Life toward resolution of truth by innate "a priori" conceptual absolutes.

Concepts, existing in Abstract Intellect in human Mind Life, exist as quality of absolute, of necessary contingency for "anything" to exist true, as secondary concepts; Spirit Ideas of earthly reality establishing broader, deeper comprehension and understanding of earthly reality perceptual experience by human body substance five senses.

Secondary concepts possess a more qualitative status of knowing earthly reality than do sense experienced primary percepts. Primary percepts are mediated, conditioned, influenced by earthly human psychological, practical, pragmatic, socio-political generic attitudes resulting in limited perceptual awareness of earthly reality.

Secondary concepts, innately "a priori" held in human Mind Life, validate primary percepts. Primary percepts "trans space" into secondary concepts, first, remaining as mental quality of "synthetic" attempting human Mind Life validation as truth. Human Mind Life cognitive mental operations metaphysically transform primary percepts into secondary concepts in cognitive order to discover truth. Human Mind Life cognitive mental operations function metaphysical cognitive processes (1) attention (focus), (2) association, (3) adaptation, (4) accommodation, (5) assimilation, and (6) application. Primary percepts reside within status of "synthetic a priori" during the mental moments when cognitive awareness is attempting to coalesce in attempt to validate as believable the primary percept transforming primary percept into a tenacious secondary concept. Human Mind Life innate "a priori" knowledge validates the primary percept. The primary concept no longer resides in mental status of "synthetic." Primary percept has now transformed into a secondary concept as new "a priori" knowledge believed in human Mind Life. Secondary concepts come to exist in human Mind Life as intellectual evidence.

Sensible intuition. A consideration of how we know in regards to the nature of knowledge was given philosophical speculation by Gottfried Leibniz, (1646-1716), in his **New Essays on Human Understanding**, suggesting that "sensible intuition" about "anything" was merely having a "sense" about it, and, not knowledge of it.

"The senses, although they are necessary for all our actual knowledge, are not sufficient to give us the whole of it, since the senses never give anything but instances, that is to say particular or individual truths. Now all the instances which confirm a general truth, however numerous they may be, are not sufficient to establish the universal necessity of this same truth, for it does not follow that what happened before will happen in the same way again... From which it appears the necessary truths, such as we find in pure mathematics, and particularly, in arithmetic and geometry, must have principles whose proof does not depend on instances, nor consequently on the testimony of the senses..." (Preface, pp.150-151).

Sensible intuition equals sense awareness as a quality of self-awareness. How do I "seem" myself within earthly reality." "I attempt to find out." Earthly human in earthly reality sense experiences anything____what is it____how do I react to the "anything." "Will my perception, impression, opinion, earthly reality invalidated sense intuition, about sense experiencing it, enrich me, enhance me?" "Do I care?" "Am I driven by this sensible experience of earthly reality?" "How much do I know in social order to successfully react to this earthly reality provocation?" "Do I care?" Actually, my earthly reality sense intuition is simply to walk away!"

Does the sense experience with an earthly reality "haunt" my earthly reality quality sense intuition, (guess) to pursue it? "My earthly reality quality sense intuition tells me to walk away." "My self-awareness, my earthly reality quality sense intuition (guess), tells me that I do not care, nor, am I driven, by this earthly reality provocation."

Nevertheless, either (1) I am forced pro formed to react "to my gut feeling" in selfish vanity in social order to confirm that my earthly reality quality sense intuition was correct, or, (2) I am forced pro formed to react to the earthly reality situation because of "self" in the circumstance within earthly reality situation, or, (3) my human Mind Life intellectual intuition exists that I need to force pro form good, and, to reconcile evil with good, as conscience conscious awareness principle. I am the one who chooses! Do I use human body substance "sensible intuition" of my sense experiences in social order "to take a guess?" Or, do I refer to my intellectual intuition to tell me truth?

Earthly reality quality of synthetic sense intuition, human residual animalistic instincts, gives to earthly human, a "sense" of earthly reality but not knowledge of earthly reality, because, although I may be only sense experiencing an earthly reality quality of sense intuition, "(1) I do not posses necessary contingency knowledge of the situation and the circumstances, (2) logical reason speaks more loudly to me than does physical sense experience, (3) "good" speaks louder to me than does "evil," (4) my Mind Life "a priori" insightful foreknowledge speaks louder to me than does some "a posteriori" synthetic, pathetic, egotistical earthly reality situation.

Animals rely upon instinct____as a safe-guarding gift. Intellectual intuition can be foresightful and insightful____at that mental moment, intellectual intuition is not based and biased upon human body substance immediate, unthoughtful reaction having an earthly reality quality sense intuition_____similar to an animal behaving instinctually. Existing as a safe-guarding gift to human Mind Life, intellectual intuition is not a sense reaction; intellectually understood human Mind Life intuition now becomes quality of intellectual discernment. Human Mind Life listens to intellectually validated intellectual evidence as intellectual intuition.

What knowledge, reacting as discerning intellectually validated intuition is, can, only become defined by the human Mind Life that stores only believed, intellectually validated knowledge, and, uses believed, intellectually validated knowledge to effect and to affect cognitive and psychological homeostasis outcome. Relying upon human body substance five senses deceive relatively and uncertainly.

Sensibility as Intellectual Intuition exists as a quality of Practical Intellect pragmatic and practical mental operations by which Practical Intellect has acquired quality practical and pragmatic perceptual awareness in sensible order to force pro form acute, confident self-awareness ability within free will accordance toward meaningful measure of kindness, respect, and empathy, alongside virtue of prudent wisdom to intelligently sensibly react to earthly reality circumstantial situations. Knowledge begets virtue; virtue begets wisdom. ***Sensibility as Intellectual Intuition requires intellectual discernment. Intellectual intuition exists as intellectually astute faculty of cognitive understanding using pre-existing knowledge in cognitive order to contemplate pre-existing knowledge in cognitive order to extend to sensible intuition logical reasoning of any sense perception, sense impression, sense opinion of sensible intuition. Sensible intuition tends to constrain any settlement of resolution___ because sensible intuition only "seems" (guesses) "what that is?" Intellectual intuition immediately, spontaneously, autonomously "knows" "what that is?"***

Sensibility as Phronesis existed for the Ancient Greeks as a metaphysical idea within philosophical speculation as ***practical wisdom***. For the Ancient Greeks, phronesis was sensible intuition using practical intelligence____not using sense perception, seems impression, sense opinion gained from sense experience of earthly reality. Practical Intellect took "mental moments" in social practical and pragmatic order to discern prudent phronesis_____what to do, how to do it, in social order to cause the least harm, to achieve a common good for the most, in social order to achieve, for, the most, impartial outcome.

Sensibility as Wisdom exists as a very sagacious cognitive level of cognitive awareness. Wisdom can extend wisdom as intellectual intuition even into earthly reality quality of sense intuition in cognitive praxis as a gift given as the virtue of innate knowing of insightful immediate, spontaneous, autonomous cognitive knowing of "what to empathetically do when to do it." ***Wisdom*** exists as ultimate innate knowledge of intellectual intuition which causes the effect of the virtuous praxis of wisdom. ***Wisdom*** exists as cognitive recognition and realization of ultimate innate knowledge of intellectual intuition. ***Wisdom*** exists as cognitive recognition and realization of ultimate innate knowledge of Human Nature.

Sensibility as Virtue. Aristotle explained ***virtue*** at its best in his book, **Nicomachean Ethics**   praxis of virtue is at its best when human Mind Life understands at the right time, about the right things, towards the right people, for the right end, and, in the right way intellectual intuition of how to empathically spontaneously and autonomously behave and what to say in an immediate earthly reality space and time.

Set groups is a sociological term used to distinguish, without any socially intended prejudice or bias, similar physiological characteristics existing within sociologically defined set groups.

Sign exists as a conventionally accepted representational linguistic, mathematical, figurative, or gestural symbol system earthly conventionally construed within alphabetical, mathematical, figurative, or gestural configurations as an attempt to metaphysical representational interact metaphysical thought as socio-cultural significance within the sign system with earthly human personalized systems of meaning individualized idiosyncratically within earthly human systems of reality, systems of truth, and systems of belief. Sign exists as a conventionally accepted representational symbol system enabling earthly humans to abstract meaning from concrete-empirical stimuli by means of sense experience and sense perception____more-or-less commensurate with each other. Sign exists as a conventionally accepted representational symbol system that enables human Mind Life to transcendentally acquire meaningful measure from earthly reality. Concrete-empirical sign transcendentally translates into abstract symbolic meaning idiosyncratic quality of individualized, personal, and idiosyncratic system of reality, system of truth, system of belief. A concrete-empirical sign system symbolizes possibility of personalized, idiosyncratically transformed meaning acquisition into human Mind Life. A concrete-empirical sign system facilitates human Mind Life to attempt to share "significance" as meaning in earthly reality.

Signify connotes meaning. Signs and symbols represent possibilities of abstracting meaning from sense experiencing earthly reality. Signs and symbols are intended to represent a "generic" meaning, however, when the sign or the symbol "translates" meaning by "significance of symbol," human Mind Life metaphysical thought, "meaning" translates into mysterious tremendums (Joseph Campbell).

Situation becomes the content-filled and context-filled space or point in time in earthly reality when non- objective earthly reality information exists no longer able to objectively define an earthly human earthly reality event.

Skepticism exists within earthly human attitude when neither Practical Intellect nor Abstract Intellect possess sufficient "a priori" knowledge in cognitive order to overcome doubt or denial. Skepticism exists within earthly human attitude as a status of apprehension. Apprehension may exist within human Mind Life mental operations as a provocation toward a mental awarenesses. Apprehension may exist within human Mind Life mental operations as a fear of a mental awarenesses. Apprehension may exist within human Mind Life mental operations as an emotive reaction toward mental awarenesses. Apprehension may occur within any of these three statuses of human Mind Life mental operations interaction with human Mind Life mental awarenesses functioning as Practical Intellect and as Abstract Intellect cannot come to cognitively discern human Mind Life mental awarenesses with present interaction amongst both intellects, ego psyche, and earthly reality. Intellect apprehends that earthly reality is winning.

Social awareness: Every man walks around earthly reality with a social awareness greater than his conscious awareness. Social awareness, sociologically labeled as "social awareness," remains grounded within a socio-cultural perceptual awareness, as well as a social "generic attitude." Perceptual awareness exists as a status within practical intellect and within psyche awareness as a mental status when psyche awareness is attempting to function as the facilitator between that which human body substance is sense experiencing at a given time in space in earthly reality with that which human Mind Life metaphysically conceives as metaphysical concepts of earthly reality. Perceptual awareness cannot void itself of psyche awareness. Perceptual awareness attempts some cognitive qualification with intellectual evidence because neither perceptual awareness nor psyche awareness cognitively validate with that which human Mind Life metaphysically conceives of earthly reality. There cannot exist any perceptual awareness without human body substance, or, without human Mind Life. There cannot exist any perceptual awareness without psyche awareness. Perceptual awareness exists as more than just human body substance organ brain "sensing" human body substance as an "ego" in an earthly reality. Social awareness exists grounded within human body substance sense experiencing and sense perceiving earthly reality_____perceptual awareness and psyche awareness lack human Mind Life conscious awareness of both cognitive perceptual awareness and cognitive psyche awareness. Social awareness is grounded in earthly reality socio-political, secular culture social awareness generic attitude_____and sees no other_____

Both social awareness and perceptual awareness seek to validate "ego" (unique persona) existing in earthly reality.

Human Mind Life cognitive metaphysical concepts of "what is a social awareness" denotes that Everyman "should" become metaphysically conceptually aware of that which Carl Jung suggested as the "collective consciousness" of a social humankind_____as a social awareness of good faith in common. Instead social awareness connotes that significance that "my ego alone" "ought to" become satisfied by a secular society."

Social consciousness, as status of a conscious experience of secular society, exists as an earthly human personal, idiosyncratic socio-political, cultural secular perception, impression, opinion of society; or may exist as an earthly human personal idiosyncratic cognitive bias of that which a society should be_____secularly socio-politically cultured.

Social fact. Emile Durkheim, (1858-1917), proposed that the goal of sociology as science needed to rely only upon factual information as observed from social realities, not upon laws of nature, and, certainly not upon theological or metaphysical concepts of natural law. Factual information could come to be explained as "social fact," and then, could be considered as social scientific, objective knowledge, but, needed to be stripped of all metaphysical abstractions or philosophical speculative tautologies... as well as individual, idiosyncratic perceptions of externally existing realities... and, as well as... any human conscious awareness. Durkheim suggested that, within this complex societal, materialistic, secular evolution of mankind which came to cause man "to fore give" (give up) his moral conscience, mind in society collectively came to develop "a social awareness of a moral density." But for Durkheim, this "moral density" now must become sociologically recognized as "a social fact," or, a social phenomena! For Durkheim this "moral density" existed as a "social fact," and, not as any "conscious awareness" capable of "a transcendental moral conscience."

Sociocentric thought exists within a sociocentric quality of two realms of the possibility of collective thought: (1) the quality of the thought of earthly human contributing to (2) the social collective thought within the collectivism of a society. The collectivism of a society's thought is based and biased within political and economic information as available and as presented to the collective society_____by whom? In the case that majority of earthly human thought remains egocentric, that majority of earthly human perceive, without regard for "common good," that the society should primarily benefit them, then, quality of sociocentric thought remains egocentric. In the case that quality of majority of earthly human thought acquire a social awareness of "common good," willing to give service toward the "worthiness" of society, instead of society contributing toward their personal earthly reality "well being," then sociocentric thought may achieve a workable "fair" society.

Socialism exists as some earthly humans' earthly reality quality of "these elitist" sense perceptions, sense impressions, sense opinions of earthly reality. Ideology of Democracy affords Everyman permission to establish his owned system of earthly reality, his owned system of truth of earthly reality, his owned system of belief of earthly rightly as earthly human spontaneously and autonomously inalienably free. Earthly human inalienable freedom can not be given or taken away.

"Something" mysterious tremendous exists within metaphysical human Mind Life as metaphysical human Mind Life comes to recognize and to realize the common conceptual prototypes, archetypes, categories, principles, attributes innate to essence of humanness Human Nature becoming Human Nature potentiality and Human Nature actuality.

Space. Earthly reality discernment of "what is earthly reality space" may be give three metaphysical ontological and epistemological discernments____(1) earthly reality empirical space, (2) earthly reality rational space, and, (3) earthly reality psychological space. Space exists as an innate "a priori" absolute metaphysical concept in human Mind Life, otherwise earthly human could neither "perceive," nor, "conceive" "space."

Earthly reality ***Empirical Space*** is defined by Classical Mechanics____ now to be redefined by Quantum Mechanics. Earthly reality space is usually scientifically measured within three demissions____height, width, length. Quantum Mechanics is discerning that there exist more than three dimensions in space. Quantum Mechanics has discerned that space and time are a coalesced spacetime continuum. However, there exists no space or time in human metaphysical Mind Life; therefore human Mind Life must "trans space and time" existing in earthly reality. Descartes' speculation concerning the communicative relationship between human body substance and human Mind Life results itself as a metaphysical dualism. Human body substance could not even function without a metaphysical Mind Life.

Rational Space, according to metaphysician, Immanuel Kant, exists metaphysically conceptually___human Mind Life "conceives" concept of space and time in earthly reality order that earthly human can earthly reality order earthly human experience of earthly reality existence. Metaphysical concepts of space and time exist innately "a priori" in human Mind Life; earthly reality physical measure of space and time exist "synthetically a posteriori" in earthly reality. In earthly reality, measure of space and time exist relative to the "perceiver" (Einstein); in human Mind Life metaphysical concepts of space and time everlastingly exist absolute never to be conditioned or qualified by earthly reality relative perception of space and time.

Psychological Space exists relative to human ego psyche. Two earthly humans, at the same time in the same space in earthly reality, will never perceive his self space and time ever the same as the other does.

Space and Time. In earthly reality there is no absolute; only in human Mind Life exists absolutes everlastingly.

Speculation exists within scientific method as an hypothesis or a theory, speculation exists with social paradigm as speech acts toward acculturated influence within population thinking. Speculation exists within philosophical thought as potentiality of possibility of actuality. Speculation within scientific method and within social paradigm gives consideration toward "what is." Speculation within philosophic thought brings forth contemplation of that which "should be."

Speech does not exist as one of the five senses as physical property within body substance. Speech requires quality of Practical Intellect thought, or, quality of human Mind Life (Abstract Intellect) metaphysical thought, otherwise, speech, void of metaphysical thought, speech only allows human body substance to emit sound.

Speech acts are intentional linguistic performances that may effect and affect a listener by means of how the speech act is performed. J.L.Austin, (1911-1960), suggested that speech acts can come to "socially" change earthly reality. J.L.Austin suggested that speech acts possess three qualities: the locutionary, the illocutionary, and the perlocutionary.

Spirit ideas exist innately "a priori" in human Mind Life. ***Spirit Ideas*** exist as metaphysical sublime pro transformations, given gifts, in cognitive order for earthly human existing in an earthly reality to come to know, comprehend, understand, reasonably moral a Human Nature existing in an earthly reality. Human Nature comes into existence with human Mind Life. Human body substance comes into earthly existence biologically and physiologically designed physical matter. Human body substance will decay and die. Human Mind Life, once human Mind Life comes into earthly existence, remains everlasting as an intelligently designed essence of "being" a Human Nature, defined by Human Nature's very own "given gifts" of ***Spirit Ideas.*** While Human Nature essence exists within an earthly reality, Human Nature recognizes and realizes human Mind Life, enabling Human Nature to come to know Human Nature existing in an earthly reality as a unique persona. Unique persona metaphysically cognitively develops human Mind Life, using earthly reality "backdrop," in cognitive order to become Human Nature. In earthly reality Human Nature "be's," "becoming" Human Nature in earthly reality. Unique persona relies upon the ***Spirit Ideas***, held innately "a priori" in human Mind Life, in cognitive order to become Human Nature intended intelligently designed Human Nature. ***Spirit Ideas*** hold the truth ideal of "what is (be's) Human Nature. ***Spirit Ideas*** hold the truth ideal of "what and why is (be's) earthly reality.

Stimuli, physiologically, is that which exists concretely, physically external to the senses of earthly human body substance which provokes earthly human body substance toward a physical action, or, a physical reaction. Stimuli, psychologically, is that which exists concretely, physically external to earthly human body substance senses that can provoke a sense perception from a sense experience____ "what is it."

Sublime pro formations exist innately "a priori" in human Mind Life. Sublime pro formations exist as absolute, necessary, universal, and everlastingly. Sublime pro formations define Human Nature. Human Nature exists absolutely necessary, and, universally everlastingly once an earthly human has been created as Intelligent Design. Human Nature exists sublimely pro formed absolutely to Human Nature essence. Human nature essence exists as the universal everlasting absolute archetypes and prototypes that define Human Nature____truth, equal, fair, trust, honor, rectitude, probity, good, moral, reasonable. Human Nature is Human Nature, otherwise, Human Nature is not Human Nature_____any earthly existence not true to itself does not exist as itself as earthly reality existence.

Subjective exists as a psychological, practical, pragmatic mental quality to perceive events, objects, and others in such a manner that the immediate perception, impression, opinion of events, objects, others remains infected and affected by the perceptions, impressions, and opinions of the subjective earthly human.

Sustains exists within the metaphysical realm of metaphysical human Mind Life. ***Sustains*** suffers human Mind Life and comforts human Mind Life in cognitive function to acquire knowledge in cognitive order to develop intelligent awareness of knowledge.

Sustains functions as a metaphysical ability of human Mind Life to give succor and sustenance to the cognitive structure of human Mind Life intended cognitive functions. Metaphysical human Mind Life structures earthly human Practical Intellect alongside earthly human Abstract Intellect in cognitive order to function cognition, thought, percepts, concepts, language, conscious awareness, as well as multitudes of mental awarenesses; to function abstraction, cognitive attention, accommodation, assimilation, adaptation, and application of human Mind Life metaphysical thought and metaphysical language in cognitive relationship to earthly reality profane disrespect for earthly reality very existence. Human Mind Life develops abstraction of concepts, comprehension of human Mind Life concepts relationship to earthly reality percepts, an understanding in depth and broad of the ontology and the teleology of "why" existence. Reason develops as the "grand sustain" of obeisant reverence for "why" existence.

Symbol exists as a linguistic, mathematical, or figurative "sign," which, "sign" has (1) socio-culturally come to represent, or symbolize," a conventionally accepted "significance," or, (2) individually has come to individualize a "significance" of an individualized, idiosyncratic abstract meaning.

Syntax is the consideration of the rules that have been established within a conventionally agreed upon system of language in social order to form words into sentences that may connote or denote propositions of declarative, interrogative, and exclamatory statements. Language formulated into syntax as a grammatical representation of the declarative, interrogative, or exclamatory proposition remain only "as words on a page," or, "sound heard" unless these words, whether syntactically formulated or not, are given meaning by some quality of intellectual evidence acquired or expressed as metaphysical thought. Placement of signs and symbols into "ultimate" syntax may assist in comprehension, however, quality of metaphysical thought and intelligence has greater significance upon "meaning" than does sign, symbol, or syntax. In the consideration of linguistic speculation "of dependency grammar" by Lucien Tesniere, (1893-1954) language usage of "predicate" dependency within syntax aids in analytical logical thinking which uses language as its artificer. Analysis, or, analytical logical thinking, defines the linguistic mentally operational process within logical thought of abstractly "deconstructing" the logical proposition into its constituent parts in logical thought order to discern the "essential" attributes and qualities necessary to make up the "actual" possibility (existence) of the idea. Grammar as linguistic structure does give functional reliability toward logical language expression. Grammar as linguistic structure builds the meaning of the sentence around the "subject" and the "predicate." In order to discern meaning from the sentence, logical thought "seeks out" the "subject" and the "predicate," first, and then, establishes the functional reliability of the syntactical grammar toward discovery of meaning. "What is the, if any, meaning relationship to the subject and the predicate?" Language stimulates analytical logical thinking by means of syntactical grammar.

Theoretical speculation may be given consideration to the structure and function of language when language exists as abstract, metaphysical thought in human Mind Life. While human Mind Life uses metaphysical language in cognitive order to discern possibilities of "existence in thought" in cognitive order to discern meaning and to resolve contradictions, to make judgments and to make decisions, to interact thought, does metaphysical language in human Mind Life, thinking of and by itself, necessarily use grammatical syntax? Does metaphysical thought using metaphysical language "think" relationship of absolute concept to absolute concept?

Synthetic a priori proposition comes to exist within human Mind Life mental operations within those "mental moments" when a synthetic a posteriori proposition has been placed "in abeyance" awaiting validation by "a priori (innate) knowledge" (Plato) held within intellectual evidence within metaphysical Mind Life.

Synthetic a priori propositions are mathematical propositions expressed within mathematical symbol systems. For example, the concept "12" is not contained in the concept of "7" or the concept of "5." Concepts and meanings of numbers are learned a posteriori, however, once mathematical concepts are learned, these mathematical concepts "a priori" permit continued acquisition of knowledge "a posteriori"... therefore, mathematical propositions, Kant labeled, "synthetic a priori propositions."

Synthetic a posteriori proposition exist within Practical Intellect mental operations as earthly reality information "synthetic a posteriori." Synthetic "a posteriori" propositions present Practical Intellect mental operations with constant contradiction because absolute "a priori" concepts, held in Abstract Intellect, as intellectual evidence, cannot validate synthetic a posteriori proposition earthly reality (information) as true. At human Mind Life "mental moments" when synthetic "a posteriori" propositions cannot be validated by human Mind Life absolute "a priori" concepts, Practical Intellect synthetic "a posteriori" propositions are mentally operationally placed into "abeyance" awaiting validation or non-validation. Practical Intellect ego psyche synthetic "a posteriori" proposition has been perceived as an "anything earthly reality uncertain" existing in earthly reality, a sense perception of a sense experience attempting meaning and value as possibly accepted intellectual evidence. Practical Intellect synthetic "a posteriori" proposition mentally operationally transforms into Abstract Intellect synthetic "a priori" proposition while awaiting intellectual validation by human Mind Life as cognitive process of mental operations within human Mind Life. Human Mind Life cognitive processes using intellectual evidence may validate the synthetic "a prior" proposition transforming the synthetic "a priori" proposition into human Mind Life "a priori" knowledge meaningful and valuable enriching and enhancing human Mind Life renewed conscious awareness of phenomenal earthly reality.

Synthetic proposition "a posteriori" can be a statement of thought expressed by means of earthly reality language or mathematical symbol system that validates itself "a posteriori." All earthly reality synthetic propositions require sense experience and sense perception for justification as earthly reality explanation of sense perception of sense experience. An example of a synthetic "a posteriori" proposition states: "Some bachelors are unhappy." An earthly reality synthetic "a posteriori" proposition is a statement whose predicate explains its subject. "Some bachelors are unhappy," or, "many bachelors are unhappy" would require observation of earthly reality "bachelors" in earthly order to justify the statement. Synthetic propositions "a posteriori" require sense experience and sense perception in earthly order to justify the statement by means of "inferential induction."

Synthesis occurs within human Mind Life mental operations can bring forth renewed conscious awareness resolving contradiction between that which Abstract Intellect holds as innate "a priori" intellectual evidence (knowledge) with that which ego psyche holds as "a posteriori" perceptual evidence of earthly reality.

System is a mental operational categorizing of recognized characteristics as universals as manifested in perceived earthly reality which enables a mental formation of a collective unity of thought of specific, yet, associated concepts, possibly collaborated absolute concepts. Difficulty in making a system "worthy" arises when the system is dehumanized. "Worthy" systems become dependent upon individualized systems of earthly reality, systems of truth, systems of belief that arbitrarily determine "how" the system theory "should be" organized. Although a system theory is seeking a collective unity of specific concepts, earthly human perceptions deceive possibility of universal conceptions of system. The only "worthy" system is the human Mind Life conceptual system. Earthly humans mind Life recognize, then, expect, certain earthly reality characteristics as universally humanly appropriated. For example, in a restaurant, I like MY waiter to pay attention to "ME," I like My food appropriately presented, hot, and, in sequence of My eating the courses... I want individualized attention, not a system of food runners. In a remodel project, I do not want individual task workers who attend to their specific expertise and give no regard toward other tasks workers, all of whom need to co-ordinate every task within each's copious detailing in task order that the end results perfect. Systems that become dehumanized will not become "worthy" systems. What is the human element in a Systems Theory? The goal of a System Theory is to make the human element irrelevant; the goal of a system Theory is to make the human element not threatening to the System Theory. There exist no better System Theory than the human Mind Life.

Systems Theory suggests that the use of interdisciplinary transdisciplinary systems of scientific investigation, observing the interrelationships of the interactions occurring within various scientific systems of activity, that may come to benefit any one specific scientific discipline. Use of systems theory may come to benefit individual scientific systems such as psychology, sociology, anthropology, political science, economics, social engineering when each individual discipline interrelates itself with earthly reality information held by the other disciplines. The goal of each individual discipline is to better understand earthly human behaviors. Systems Theory suggest that each individual discipline of scientific investigation may come to benefit the other. There exist no better System Theory than the human Mind Life.

Systems Theories identify and define the structures and the functions as structures and functions relate to and interact within the system, or, as structures and functions of one system interact with another system. Systems theories might look into the structures and the functions of mental operations existing as physical human brain, or, might look into the structures and the functions of mental operations as metaphysical human intellect. Systems theories might look into the human interaction amongst personal and idiosyncratic systems of reality, systems of truth, and systems of belief. Systems theories might look into the human interaction amongst human intellects, ego psyche, and earthly reality. Systems theories might be used as investigation into any inorganic social, political, economic, scientific disciplines or organizations. Contemporary system of belief in science, in the social sciences, and in secular humanism presently only look into inorganic systems of social, political, economic, and scientific disciplines and organizations as system theory that these inorganic systems have inorganic ability to structure, function, and maintain themselves void of human Mind Life.

TELEONOMY referred to biologically based goal-directed mental functions, existing as mental property in human body substance, that come to exist due to natural selection of genetic variability, and not to any relationship with human Mind Life conscious awareness, or, any supernatural guidance, or, any possibility of human free will. Any possibility of mental functions, existing in mental property within human body substance, were to be scientifically considered as "biologically" goal-directed functions, void of all notion of human free will and human intelligent design, however, any possibility of mental functions were "cosmically naturally selected non-randomly organically biologically?!" Teleonomy contrasts with Aristotle's teleology. Contemporary science suggests a "scientific" explanation for "final cause." Aristotle, in his notion of Teleology, suggested a "metaphysical" notion of "final cause." Final cause, for Aristotle, necessarily existed because human Mind Life needed "to know why, and, what." Who am I? Where am I? Where did I come from____even if, as a biological random happenstance event. (Author's note: this author cannot believe that a human would believe that human came from a biological random happenstance event without cause or purpose, when human Mind Life always seeks out cause and purpose for anything earthly existing, especially when the anything earthly remains in status of "anything earthly uncertain!")

Aristotle's "final cause" gave philosophic speculation toward explanation "by virtue of the reason" why something exists and does what it does. Aristotle's teleology suggested that just as everything existing within nature has "reason for existence" and was directed by purpose of its "reason," the same "natural essence" existed in human. Teleonomy suggested that natural selection became dependent upon hindsight and not foresight. Teleonomy suggested that human body physical substance, and, human body substance "mental" physical organ brain evolved by means of natural selection, which natural selection over time, by process of adaptation, necessarily "alters" genotype and phenotype due to sense experience sense perceiving that some human behaviors resulted as "unworkable and insufficient." Kind of a brain "trail and error" that "mechanistically, biologically operates human body substance mental substance organ brain in biological order to correct human body substance mental substance organ brain's previous mistakes." A basic premise of teleonomy is that human body substance mental substance organ brain works more or less as a computer mechanism that "aims at a determined goal," or, is "goal-directed" by nature of the functions existing within biological genotype interacting with biological phenotype. Teleonomy redefined Aristotle's teleology. In notion of Teleonomy any possible mental functions existing in human body substance are biologically determined.

Theory, existing within dynamic state of hypothesis, does not become belief until human Mind Life has intellectually validated present existing "a priori" knowledge with any newly acquired "a posteriori" sense experience, observation, experiment, or inferential induction of the earthly reality synthetic propositional theory toward possibility of cognitive inclusion into human Mind Life belief system____nevertheless, scientific theories proofs will always remain, within earthly reality, as possibility of "reverse proof" (Karl Popper). Karl Popper, (1902-1994), explained that a scientific hypothesis may be scientifically proven as "proof positive," while, at the same time be scientifically proven as "proof negative." Thomas Kuhn, (1922-1996), in his book, **The Structure of Scientific Revolutions**, explained that social scientific paradigms are always dynamically changing their hypothesis in what Kuhn referred to as "paradigm shifts." Albert Einstein, (1879-1955), explained the Theory of Relativity. Max Planck, (1858-1947), the originator of Quantum Theory, explained that Plank's physics quanta constant always remained a variable. Warner Heisenberg, (1901-1976), explained that within mathematical measurement there always exists an Uncertainty Principle. Human Mind Life intelligent "meaningful measure" everlastingly positively develops. Theory remains as scientific or philosophic or metaphysical speculation within earthly reality.

Theory establishes a synthetic propositional speculation of the possibility of a new empirical perception, or as a possibility of a new theoretical conception. Theory builds upon empirical perception using theoretical conception. Theory, whether existing toward scientific empirical discovery, or, existing toward philosophic speculation, holds intent toward the resolution of an outcome. The use of theory toward resolution of contradictions coming to exist in thought, due to conflict between empirical perception and theoretical conception, is not a phenomena limited to scientific method. The use of theory toward resolution of contradictions coming to exist in thought, due to conflict between empirical perception and theoretical conception, becomes to exist within the metaphysical realm of the possibility of thought. The use of theory toward resolution of contradictions presented by perception's absurdities toward reconciliation with intellectual evidence becomes a basic thinking process intellect uses to establish his system of reality, system of truth, and system of belief. Use of earthly reality Critical

Theory attacking earthly reality produces negative worldview as hopeless earthly reality.

Theoretical speculation may be given consideration to the structure and to the function of earthly reality language when earthly reality language transcendently transforms into human Mind Life metaphysical abstract thought, now thought in human Mind Life, as metaphysical absolute, universally beholding language__never conditioned to anything earthly reality specific. Human Mind Life uses earthly reality language in cognitive order to discern truth possibilities of human Mind Life thought in cognitive order to discern meaning and to resolve contradictions as validating that human Mind Life innately "a priori" metaphysically recognizes and realizes, in cognitive order, intellectual ability to make intelligent judgments, and, to make intelligent decisions, as intellectually meaningfully measured against earthly reality perceptually measured observation of earthly reality. Earthly reality information gives no theoretical consideration toward earthly reality situation and circumstance____earthly reality information gives consideration to earthly reality situational and circumstantial practical and pragmatic earthly reality "real" practical and pragmatic earthly reality specific, non-universal, non-objective situations and circumstances. Theoretical speculation "imagines" the possibility of a "should be" universally applied actuality.

Theoretical thought or thoughtful speculation within mental operations comes to exist as a quality of dynamic speculation, theory, or hypothesis, intention provoked by scientific observation, experiment, data collecting and/or philosophically reasoned speculation due to mentally operational contradiction recognized and realized between the two systems of thinking____scientific empirical or philosophically reasoned. Theoretical thought or thoughtful speculation comes to be provoked as a result of the biases recognized and realized within (1) sense perception of sense experiences, (2) earthly reality quality sensible intuition, (3) perceptual evidence, (4) intellectual evidence, (5) possibility and potentiality within Abstract Intellect's cognitive awareness of quality of cognitive function of the understanding.

Thinking exists as a faculty of mind functioning within the cognitive structure of intellect.

Thinking exists as the use of intellect within logical thought both innately "a priori" and earthly reality "a posteriori." Thinking using logical thought earthly reality "a posteriori" uses cognitive functions in cognitive order to acquire knowledge from sense experience and sense perception. Thinking using logical thought innately "a priori" uses cognitive functions to accommodate, assimilate, and resolve contradictions existing between primary intellect and abstract intellect. Thinking becomes the function of the use of thought. Thinking exists as the intellect "metaphysically recognizing and realizing itself." Thought comes to exist as the intellect "metaphysically realized." Intellect, thinking, and thought transcendentally, metaphysically sustain each other. Metaphysically "embodied" intellect results as the "culmination" of thought's ability to abstract concepts from percepts.

Thinking exists as the use of intellect using thought both earthly reality "a posteriori" and innately "a priori." Human Mind Life innate thinking transforms acquired primary percepts earthly reality "a posteriori" into acquired secondary concepts "a priori" in cognitive, abstract process of thinking. Transformational thinking requires the mental operations of abstraction, cognitive awareness, (and the seven mental operations existing within the mental operation of cognitive awareness), comprehension, understanding, and reason within the use of practical intellect and the use of abstract intellect. Because the thinking process, within the process of transformational thinking, evokes human Mind Life mental operations, which provoke, or demand, cognitive validation of sense perception of sense experience with existing human Mind Life intellectual evidence toward new abstract concept development. Human Mind Life cognitive functions of reflection, analysis, and synthesis come into play. Conscious awareness integrates human Mind Life mental processes of reflection, analysis, and synthesis within human Mind Life cognitive process of thinking. Thinking existing as the use of intellect within logical thought cognitive innately "a priori" can be developed and perfected earthly reality "a posteriori" by means of "sensibility" sense perception of sense experience of earthly reality.

Thought development becomes a human Mind Life cognitive mental operational process of primary percepts interfacing secondary concepts developing human Mind Life cognition. Thought development becomes human Mind Life sequential and incremental intellectual developmental mental operational activity of attention (focus), associative learning, association, adaptation (resolution), accommodation, assimilation, acquisition, and application of primary percepts interfacing with secondary concepts, and, of intellectual mental processes of cognitive awareness, of the comprehension, and, of the understanding toward conscious awareness of meaningful measure of concept awareness, of thought awareness, of language awareness, of intellectual awareness. Human Mind Life thought begins development as socio-political, cultural interrelationship of qualities of ego psyche quality of perceptual, impressionable, opinionated thought. Ego psyche socio-political, cultural thought becomes qualified by earthly human multiple psychological quality perceptions, impressions, and opinions of earthly reality. Innate conscious awareness of necessity to survive in earthly reality initiates cognitive thought development in human Mind Life in earthly human.

Earthly human psychological quality perceptions, impression, opinions of earthly reality begin to qualify socio-political cultural thought. Does an earthly human "believe" the earthly reality socio-political, cultural information that earthly human perceives, acquires as quality of earthly reality impressions and of quality of earthly reality opinions of sense experiencing earthly reality____does limited earthly reality socio-political, cultural quality of earthly reality information as perceptions, impressions, opinions become an earthly human's "believable" knowledge____become a very limiting earthly reality knowledge? Does an earthly human "believe" that the perceptions, impressions and opinions of sense experiences of earthly reality form quality of thought development, concept development, language development, intellectual development, conscious awareness of an earthly human merely surviving in an earthly reality? Do earthly human perceptions, impressions, opinions of earthly reality establish earthly human system of reality, system of truth, system of belief? Does learning mathematics, science, literature, prose, poetry, music, dance, song, ritual, story, reading a Great Book, enrich, enhance an earthly human Mind Life thought development? Can an earthly human acquire a human Mind Life the thinks thought psychologically, socially, and intellectually qualified with depth of cognitive comprehension, with depth of the understanding of human Mind Life cognition quality? By reading this sentence thought was developed in your Mind Life.

Thoughtful significance or symbolic significance within human Mind Life mental operations comes to exist as a quality within abstract intellect's cognitive awareness of the cognitive function of the understanding. The cognitive awareness of the cognitive function of the understanding allows abstract intellect to think using thought as linguistic conceptual symbolism void of any and all perceptual evidence held within practical intellect. Conceptual thought is not using any contextual, situational perception of earthly reality object, event, or other. Thought is using thought, of and by itself, as the conceptual essence of the possible essential reality of object event, or other. Thought uses linguistic symbolism (conceptual metaphysical language) in cognitive order to achieve thoughtful significance toward acquiring knowledge-for-the-sake-of-knowledge alone void of any and all sense perception of sense experience.

Transcendence requires human Mind Life mental operations to ignore earthly time in earthly space____to "Trans Space"____and "Trans Time." "Trans space" exists when mental moments within human Mind Life mental operations transcend earthly human existence notions of "space" and "time." "Mental moments" existing within human Mind Life mental operations necessarily, by virtue of the essence of their function, place sense perception into suspension, because, while sense experience exists within earthly human body substance existing in earthly reality of time and space, sense perception initiates human Mind life mental operations that demand "thinking." Due to provocation by perception human Mind Life mental operations must now react to earthly human body substance. Human Mind Life mental operations react to earthly human body substance by the process of "thinking." Thinking exists as a faculty of human Mind Life innately "a priori" functioning within the cognitive structure of human Mind Life intellect. Thinking exists as the use of human Mind Life intellect within thought both innately "a priori" and earthly reality "a posteriori." Thinking using thought earthly reality "a posteriori" uses human Mind Life cognitive functions in cognitive order to acquire knowledge form sense perception of sense experience. Thinking using thought innately "a priori" uses cognitive functions to accommodate, assimilate, and resolve contradictions existing between Practical Intellect and Abstract Intellect. Thinking becomes the function of the use of metaphysical thought. Thinking exists as human Mind Life intellect "metaphysically realizing itself." Thought comes to exist as human Mind Life intellect "metaphysically realized." Intellect, thinking thought metaphysically sustain each other. Thinking exists as the use of intellect using thought both earthly reality "a posteriori," and, innately "a priori." Transformation of Practical Intellect acquired primary percepts from earthly reality "a posteriori" into Abstract Intellect recognized and realized metaphysical secondary concepts innately "a priori" becomes human Mind Life abstract process of thinking. Transformation requires human Mind Life cognitive mental operations of abstraction, cognitive awareness, (and the seven mental operations existing within the mental operation of cognitive awareness), comprehension, understanding, and reason within the use of Practical Intellect "in correspondence" of the use of Abstract Intellect. By virtue of the essence of human Mind Life mentally operational functioning cognitive metaphysical "thinking:" (1) human Mind Life thinking exists innately "a priori," human Mind Life metaphysical thinking develops metaphysical thought in human Mind Life____developing intellect, developing thinking, developing thought, intellectually thinking knowledge as abstract, metaphysical thought, (2) intelligent thought development, process of learning, and acquisition of knowledge demand human Mind Life "to think abstractly, metaphysically" (3) thinking "abstractly metaphysically" demands human Mind Life to suspend (trans space) earthly human body substance existing within earthly time and earthly space, (4) metaphysical thinking relies upon the innate "a priori" existing cognitive mental processes of human Mind Life___human Mind Life exists metaphysically beyond any physical, (5) metaphysical human Mind Life, existing as quality of Practical Intellect, and, as quality of Abstract Intellect cognitively interact "transcendentally" with each other, (6) human Mind Life metaphysically thinking "transcendently" requires both intellects, Practical and Abstract, to "trans space" (transform) each other, (6) Practical Intellect, by virtue of essential cognitive function, "perceives" earthly reality as "anything earthly whatever pleasures ego psyche", with aid of human body substance senses experiences, (7) Abstract Intellect, by virtue of essential cognitive function "conceives" absolute metaphysical concepts about that which essential human existence is intelligently, reasonably, morally supposed to be, (8) intellects, thinking, and thought transcendently sustain each other.

Transcendental is a terminology used philosophically by Immanuel Kant and spiritually by certain Eastern religions. Transcendental quality of thought, as terminology in this manuscript, is defined as a mental status of a metaphysical thought, which metaphysical thought initially provoked human Mind Life attention (focus). Human Mind Life quality of Practical Intellect, psychologically ego psyche unconsciously unsatisfied, and, intellectually non-validated due to multitudes of earthly human ego psyche psychological perceptions, impressions, opinions of "who is human essentially existing in earthly reality" cannot neither be psychologically nor intellectually satisfied by any "anything earthly reality existing uncertain." Human Mind Life force pro forms earthly reality Practical Intellect to transcend into the Spirit Ideas innately "a priori" existing within human Mind Life.

Transformation of acquired earthly reality Practical Intellect primary percepts "a posteriori" by human Mind Life mental operations toward the recognition and the realization of innate "a priori" metaphysical secondary concepts universally initiated in earthly reality (Aristotle) develops as a human Mind Life mental operation of an abstract thinking process. Transformation requires the mental operations of abstraction, cognitive awareness, (and the seven mental operations existing within the mental operation of cognitive awareness), comprehension, understanding, and reason within the use of practical intellect and the use of abstract intellect. By virtue of the essence for human Mind Life mentally operational function of "thinking," human Mind Life metaphysical thinking innately exists "a priori," developing metaphysical thought developing intellectual cognition.

Transformation develops as a human Mind Life cognitive function of abstract process of thinking. Transformation force pro forms human Mind Life mental operations of abstraction, cognitive awareness, (and the seven mental operations existing within the mental operation of cognitive awareness), comprehension, understanding, and reason within earthly realty Practical Intellect provoking human Mind Life metaphysical function of Abstract Intellect. Because the thinking process, within the process of transformation, evokes human Mind Life mental operations which provoke, or demand, mental conscious awareness validation of sense perception of sense experience with existing human Mind Life believable knowledge toward new conceptual development, the cognitive functions of reflection, analysis, and synthesis come into play. Conscious awareness integrates the mental processes of reflection, analysis, and synthesis within human Mind Life cognitive process of thinking. Thinking existing as the use of human Mind Life intellects (Practical with Abstract) force pro formed logical thought innately "a prior"____requiring use of human Mind Life.

"Trans space" exists within human Mind Life mental moments when human Mind Life mental operations transcend earthly human existence notions of "space" and "time." "Mental moments" existing within human Mind Life mental operations necessarily, by virtue of the essence that they function, place sense perception into suspension, because, while sense experience exists within human body substance existing in earthly reality of time and space, sense perception provokes human Mind Life mental operations that demand abstract, metaphysical "thinking." Due to provocation by Practical Intellect perception, human Mind Life mental operations must now react metaphysically to human body physical substance. Human Mind Life mental operations metaphysically react to human body substance by the process of abstract, metaphysical "thinking." Abstract, metaphysical thinking exists as a cognitive faculty of human Mind Life innately "a priori" functioning within the cognitive structure of human Mind Life quality of intellects. Abstract, metaphysical thinking exists as the use of quality of intellects within abstract, metaphysical thought both earthly realty "a posterior" and innately "a priori." Abstract, metaphysical thinking "a priori" using abstract, metaphysical thought "a posteriori" uses cognitive functions in cognitive order to acquire believable knowledge form sense perception of sense experience. Abstract, metaphysical thinking using abstract, metaphysical thought innately "a priori" uses cognitive functions to accommodate, assimilate, and resolve contradictions existing between earthly Practical Intellect and innate "a priori" abstract metaphysical Abstract Intellect. Abstract, metaphysical thinking cognitively develops abstract, metaphysical thought. Abstract, metaphysical thinking cognitively develops human Mind Life intellects "metaphysically realizing Practical and Abstract Intellects." Abstract, metaphysical thought cognitively develops Practical Intellect and Abstract Intellect "metaphysically realized." Practical and Abstract Intellects, abstract, metaphysical thinking, and abstract, metaphysical thought co-relationally, metaphysically sustain each other. Abstract, metaphysical thinking develops as the use of Practical Intellect with Abstract Intellect using abstract, metaphysical thought both earthly reality "a posteriori," and, innately "a priori."

Truth becomes an earthly human personal and idiosyncratic system of reality and system of belief.

Typical becomes an earthly reality "anything" culturally accepted as the norm of contemporary dominate population thinking.

Understanding: The fourth human Mind Life level of mental operation (4) of cognitive development becomes human Mind Life mental operation of ***the understanding. Understanding*** is the process by which human Mind Life mental operations ***continues*** (after human Mind Life cognitive operation of ***the comprehension),*** the process of cognitively mentally operationally recognizing and realizing cognitive intellectual relationship between earthly reality Practical Intellect primary percepts of perceptions, impression, and opinions of earthly reality, toward innate metaphysical cognitive relationship to human Mind Life innate "a priori" absolute necessary universal secondary concepts, using human Mind Life innate "a priori" knowledge, "a priori" human Mind Life established believable knowledge, of and by itself. Human Mind Life established believable knowledge functions *the cognitive understanding* within cognitive process toward comparing previously established believable knowledge with the current earthly synthetic quality information, now existing as quality of synthetic "a priori" in human Mind Life (Kant) awaiting human Mind Life believable acceptance. In the beginning of human Mind Life cognitive process, when human Mind Life met new earthly reality synthetic quality information, that earthly reality uncertain information existed, for human Mind Life, as synthetic "a posteriori" (Kant), possibly believable, possibly not believable, because the earthly reality synthetic quality information was just that___synthetic earthly possibly believable, possibly unbelievable information qualified by multitudes of personalized, individualized perceptions, impressions, and opinions. Truth exists as absolute truth; truth can never be qualified. When "something" exists as truth, that "something" is true, of and by itself. Once "something" is qualified, the "something" is no longer itself___no longer true. Within earthly reality "anything" may be "real;" however, not of necessity true!

Human Mind Life discerned the earthly reality information as possibly believable, possibly unbelievable, and, by cognitive function of "abstractly thinking," abstractly transcended the earthly reality synthetic "a posteriori" information into human Mind Life, qualifying the earthly reality information as "synthetic "a posteriori." Within "mental moments" human Mind Life "trans spaced" earthly time and earthly space, placing earthly time and earthly space "in abeyance," "human Mind Life residing within abstract thought." Using cognitive processes human Mind Life *continues* to cognitively discern the earthly reality synthetic information presented to Human Mind Life via human body substance sense experiences which human Mind Life formed as quality of earthly reality perceptions, earthly reality impressions, earthly reality opinions about earthly reality____demanding cognitive validation as believable by human Mind Life innate "a priori" knowledge.

Continuing____human Mind Life abstractly transcends earthly reality "synthetic a posteriori" information into cognitive status of "synthetic a priori" in human Mind Life cognitive mental level of ***the comprehension.*** Human Mind Life is now in a cognitive status of ***attempting comprehension*** of the earthly reality synthetic "a posteriori" information via human Mind Life abstract mental operations_____ abstraction, association, accommodation, assimilation, acceptance within comparison and co-relation between synthetic "a posteriori" earthly reality information and current human Mind Life existing believable "a priori" knowledge_____abstractly transcending quality of earthly reality "synthetic a posteriori" transformed in human Mind Life as "synthetic a priori" quality by the ***comprehension cognitive level of human Mind Life comprehension.*** Within human Mind Life abstract mental operations of the ***comprehension,*** earthly reality information presented to human Mind Life via sense perceptions, sense impressions, sense opinions acquired by Practical Intellect bring to Abstract Intellect earthly reality "synthetic a posteriori" earthly reality information. Within "mental moments" of human Mind Life mental operations, human Mind Life places, "in abeyance," all earthly reality space and time____abstracting mentally operationally transcendently transforming quality of "synthetic a posteriori" into quality of "synthetic a priori," human Mind Life attempting truth validation of "synthetic a priori" quality of human Mind Life "knowing" into established believable human Mind Life "a priori" quality knowledge. Hegel's Nodal Line abstractly mentally operationally occurs. Practical Intellect and Abstract Intellect abstractly mentally operationally "epicycle" with each other attempting contact. Practical Intellect and Abstract Intellect abstractly mentally operationally arrive a contacts with each other only within "mental moments" of "truth contact."

Human Mind Life cognitive level of ***the comprehension*** presents to human Mind Life level of ***the understanding*** the newly cognitively validated believable knowledge. Human Mind Life cognitive level of ***the understanding*** transcendently transforms the newly acquired ***comprehended*** believable knowledge____toward enhanced and enriched renewed conscious awareness of "all of it" ____establishing believable in depth and broadened ***understanding*** voiding human Mind Life of all earthly reality perceptions, impressions, opinions. Human Mind Life speaks to humanMind Life in metaphysical absolute concepts. All earthly humans are equal because all earthly humans hold the same Human Nature____within metaphysical human Mind Life there exist no qualifications, such as sex, race, nationality, ethnicity____that only happens in a phenomenal earthly reality. ***That which makes earthly humans not equal____is the cognitive understanding.***

Universals exist as human Mind Life innate "a priori" concepts within metaphysical human Mind Life. Universals exist as the metaphysical conceptual comparative prototypes that enable human intellects to come to know "something as truth." Universals are Plato's "Forms." Universals are Carl Jung's Archetypes. Universals belonged to Aristotle. Sense perceptions of sense experiences give to earthly human perceptual evidence of a relative and uncertain phenomenal earthly reality perceived personally and idiosyncratically by each earthly human. Within earthly reality space and time, earthly human body substance sense perceptions, sense impressions, sense opinions, earthly reality exists within earthly reality circumstance and immediate situations, within contexts and contents. Earthly human needs to meet human Mind Life.

Value, within human Mind Life mental operations, exists as a quality of knowledge earthly human comes to recognize and realize as absolutely meaningful toward discovery of truth. Wisdom exists as a value virtue acquired by earthly human within earthly human conscious awareness of Human Nature's value of the understanding. Immanuel Kant stated it best____enlightenment occurs when an earthly human recognizes and realizes the understanding in human Mind Life.

Validity arrives to earthly human recognition and realization within human Mind Life mental operations when earthly human conscious awareness is cognitively able to develop cognitive balance between Practical Intellect and Abstract Intellect.

Virtue. Aristotle explained *virtue* at its best in his book, **Nicomachean Ethics**___praxis of virtue is at its best when human Mind Life understands at the right time, about the right things, towards the right people, for the right end, and, in the right way intellectual intuition of how to empathically spontaneously and autonomously behave and what to say in an immediate earthly reality space and time. *Virtue* is a metaphysical absolute faculty of human Mind Life force pro formance.

Volition exists within human Mind Life mental operations as conscious awareness of Human Nature mental operation of free will. Human Mind Life cognitively develops with earthly human lifetime_____under the direction of earthly human Mind Life free will. The meaning and value of earthly human Human Nature makes earthly human self-responsible for everything earthly human does. Self-Responsibility exercising free will demands the acquisition of a lot of knowledge. Earthly reality corrupts, ego psyche corrupts, ignorance corrupts. *Volition* is a metaphysical absolute faculty of human Mind Life force pro formance.

Will exists as meaningful and valuable earthly reality direction of human Mind Life cognitive development. *Will* is a metaphysical absolute faculty of human Mind Life force pro formance.

Wisdom exists as a very sagacious cognitive level of cognitive awareness. Wisdom can extend wisdom as intellectual intuition even into earthly reality quality of sense intuition in cognitive praxis as a gift given as the virtue of innate knowing of insightful immediate, spontaneous, autonomous cognitive knowing of "what to empathetically do when to do it." *Wisdom* exists as ultimate innate knowledge of intellectual intuition which causes the effect of the virtuous praxis of wisdom. *Wisdom* exists as cognitive recognition and realization of ultimate innate knowledge of intellectual intuition. **Wisdom** exists as cognitive recognition and realization of ultimate innate knowledge of Human Nature.

Words exist in sequence of symbols, in the English language called alphabet, that make up the language as vocabulary. Words manifest themselves as a language because (1) words are spoken or written in social and cognitive order to communicate thought, and, (2) words are relied upon as a symbolic form that is capable of representing human Mind Life thought.

Work exists as earthly human behavioral manifestation of Human Nature as Human Nature extrinsic value and as Human Nature intrinsic value. Work, as human behavior, holds intrinsic value by virtue of the reason that work exists, of necessity, as Human Nature intrinsic value manifested as human behavior. Earthly human brings forth into earthly reality cognitive awareness and human free will (self-responsibility) when earthly human works. Human Mind Life brings forth into earthly reality free will (self-responsibility), and, cognitive awareness as cognitive resolve, cognitive intention, cognitive deliberation, cognitive discernment, and cognitive judgment in human body substance form of kinetic energy. Earthly human work begins in the cradle. Human body substance holds kinetic energy that once begun becomes limitless in Mind Life, Human Body, and Spiritual Animus. Work initiates learning toward worthy intention. The force of work, as kinetic energy, initiates a potentiality toward an actuality (Aristotle). Work, as kinetic energy, exists limitless. Work manifests work extrinsically, but, work initiates work intrinsically. Work exists as an absolute truth holding meaning and value in human Mind Life. **Work** is a metaphysical absolute faculty of human Mind Life force pro formance.

Worthy exists as meaning and value in Human Mind Life in Human Nature.

Worthy represents to the human spirit "the good," "the mysterious," the sacred," "the profound."

9 781728 328348